JOHN PAUL JONES
THE PIRATE
PATRIOT

° ARMSTRONG SPERRY °

young
voyageur

Quarto is the authority on a wide range of topics.

Quarto educates, entertains and enriches the lives of our readers—enthusiasts and lovers of hands-on living.

www.quartoknows.com

© 2016 Quarto Publishing Group USA Inc.
Original text © 1953 Mrs. Armstrong Sperry
Additional material © 2006 Flying Point Press
Maps © Richard Thompson, Creative Freelancers, Inc.

First published in 1953 by Random House as John Paul Jones: Fighting Sailor. This edition published in 2016 by Voyageur Press, an imprint of Quarto Publishing Group USA Inc., 400 First Avenue North, Suite 400, Minneapolis, MN 55401 USA. Telephone: (612) 344-8100 Fax: (612) 344-8692

quartoknows.com
Visit our blogs at quartoknows.com

Voyageur Press titles are also available at discounts in bulk quantity for industrial or sales-promotional use. For details contact the Special Sales Manager at Quarto Publishing Group USA Inc., 400 First Avenue North, Suite 400, Minneapolis, MN 55401 USA.

ISBN: 978-0-7603-5230-4

10 9 8 7 6 5 4 3 2 1

Library of Congress Control Number: 2016946038

Series Design: B. Middleworth
Series Creative Director: Laura Drew
Page Layout: B. Middleworth

CONTENTS

A WORD TO THE READER

In the interest of brevity, I have invented the character called "Jared Folger." He is a composite of the many loyal and efficient officers who served in numerous ships commanded by John Paul Jones.

With this exception, the people and events in this story follow the known facts.

—Armstrong Sperry

PART OF THE N

Arctick Circle.

NEW

NORTH WALES.

NE

SOUT

A New Map of NORTH AMERICA
Shewing its Principal Divisions, Chief
Cities, Townes, Rivers, Mountains &c.

Dedicated
To His Highness WILLIAM
Duke of Glocester.

Scale of English Miles.
According to Vulgar Computation.

According to Norwood's Computation.

39

PARTS AS YET UNKNOWN.

Tract or Upper

Illinois

NEW
ALBION
discovered by
Sir Francis Drake
Anns 1577.

NEW MEXICO or

HENNEPIN'S DISCOVERY

NEW GRANADA,

Discovered
about
1540, of a barren soil and
little known.

St. Fe or New Mexico.

FLOR IDA

Possest by the Spaniards

about 1527.

Hotico R.

Chiaqua R.

Holy Ghost R.

Bay of the
Holy Ghost.

New French
Settlement.

St. Barbara

NEW
BISCAYA.

Magdalen R.

Panuco R. St. Iago
d Vallos.

St. Iuan.

Culiacan.
St. Michael

St. Martin.
Zacatecas.

Panuco.

GOLF OF

Port Gra

Tropick of Cancer.

C. St. Lucas.

Aquacara.
Guadalajara.

Compostella.

Xalisco.

Colima. Mechoacan.

Liquitlan R.

MEXI

CO
or NEW SP

Mexico.

St. John
d Vlloa.

MEXICO.

Tlascala.

Los Angelos.

Bay of Campeachy.

P. Royal.

Antequera.

Chiapa.

Conquered by the Spaniards about 1518.
It is stored with Mines of Gold and Silver.

Vera Pax.

Acapulco

Los Yorvas

PACIFICK OCEAN largely taken

Sacrificio I.

Aguatulco
Tongola I.

St. Iago d.
Guatimala.

Guaveland.

St. Salvador.

Vall

I

or the GREAT INDIAN OCEAN, Commonly

St. Michael
Amapalla I.

Point Casivina.

called by our Seamen the SOUTH SEA.

Abbreviations.
B. Bay.   Arch. See.
C. Cape. Bishops See.
I. Isle.
M. Mountain.
P. Point.
R. River.

Delin MBurg: sculpt Univ. Oxon.

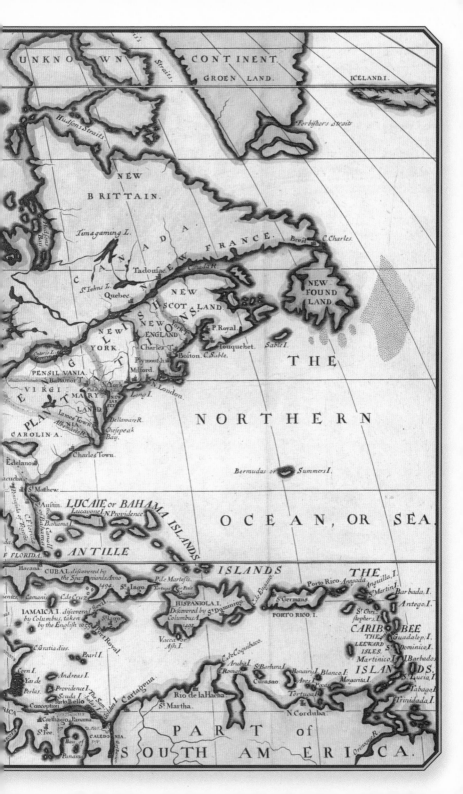

CHAPTER ONE

A PROPHECY AND A CHALLENGE

John Paul Jones. There's magic in the name! The man himself flared like a rocket across the dark and troubled times in which he lived. Born as plain John Paul, the son of a Scottish gardener, he became the confidant of statesmen and kings. He hoisted the rattlesnake flag on the first American man-of-war. He humbled the proud Royal Navy of King George and spread terror throughout the English countryside. His fame soared across land and sea. Honors were heaped upon him. The ill-fated Marie Antoinette gave him a miniature in her likeness. Great Catherine of Russia appointed him to command her Black Sea fleet. Jefferson, Washington, Benjamin Franklin called him friend.

Kilt Rock waterfall, flowing over the cliffs.

But at forty-five—ill, lonely and forgotten—he died in Paris, an exile from the beloved country of his adoption. All his life had been a fight. His unmarked grave in the St. Louis Protestant cemetery was soon buried beneath the rubble on which tradesmen built their shops. And for one hundred years its dust lay undisturbed.

Many have wondered how such a man, born a subject of the English king, could have turned his back on his native land to adopt the cause of the rebellious Colonials across the sea. Perhaps the answer to the riddle lay in John Paul's childhood—in that night when a chill wind stalked the shores of Solway Firth, and an old man spoke in bitterness of Scotland's crushing defeat at Culloden, by the Duke of Cumberland's forces.

Culloden . . . In after years, John Paul never could hear that word without flinching. The very sound of it summoned up a peat fire burning on the hearth, the drumming rain, the wind growling at the windows, and his uncle's bitter voice saying, "Culloden! Ye've always been after me to tell ye aboot it, lad."

"But you never would, Uncle."

"Nae." The word was a sigh. "These many years now I've been tryin' and tryin' to forget the disgrace of it. But this night," and the man's voice came heavily, "I'll tell ye o' Culloden, and when I'm done—ye'll understand the why."

Perhaps that was how John Paul, then a boy of twelve,

first heard of Scotland's defeat at the hands of the English king's men. He never forgot the picture of his uncle staring through the fire into the heart of a bygone battle, or the voice sorrowing, "For hours that woeful day we lay on the moor wi' our faces buried in the heather, while English bullets drilled us through and through."

"How many were there, Uncle?"

"Three thousand strong," came the proud answer. "Camerons and Robertsons, MacDonalds and Appin Stewarts. We'd trounced the English a score o' times before. It was unthinkable that we should know defeat."

"What happened? Tell me!"

The old man drew a labored breath, closed his eyes. On the hearth a charred log glowed and flamed like the tattered banners of a defeated army.

"The round-shot fell about us like hail till we could bear nae more," came the low voice. "Someone shouted an order. As one man we rose and charged. Down across the moor we roared wi' claymores swingin', and the name of Bonnie Prince Charlie burstin' in our throats. We met the English line wi' the Highland war cry and smashed it through. Ah—! Too late we discovered the trap they'd set."

"The trap, Uncle?"

"Aye, cunnin' as foxes were Cumberland's men, and we but blunderin' fools wi' a mighty love o' Scotland in our hearts."

"But you'd smashed the first line, Uncle," the boy reminded him.

"True. But back o' the first we met a second. And we,

armed only wi' broadswords and not a musket among us! Even before we could come to grips they fired their terrible volleys. Our brave clansmen fell like wheat to the scythe, mowed down, till naught but a handful was left. I among them, lucky to be alive, though I would fain a thousand times have died upon that bloody ground. Ah, woe is me!"

"Was that the end of the battle, Uncle?"

"O' the battle, yes, laddie," came the grim reply. "But only the beginnin' o' the slaughter. They hounded us through the glens. They set fire to our homes, drove off our cattle, our women and children, too. When Cumberland's men were done, the Highlands were a wasteland and have been since that day."

A damp log hissed and sputtered, filling the silence.

But all that's past these many years," the boy suggested.

"Aye, past. But not forgot. Never as long as one drop o' true blood runs in the veins of a Scot. And now Geordie—Cumberland's own nephew—sits upon the throne of England. George the Third, I'm told they call him. Hoots! A disgrace and a byword to decent-thinkin' people."

"But God makes kings as well as common men," the boy murmured.

"Aye, and *un*makes them, too. Charlie, the bonnie prince, is gone, and with him all o' Scotland's fine hopes. Ah, weel! Nae doubt ye're wonderin' why I've told ye o' this." The man was fumbling in a pocket of his jacket. He produced a water-stained envelope and bent closer to the fire. "I have by me a letter, received this day from your brother William."

John Paul's breath quickened. "From America?" he cried.

The man nodded. "William writes that the Colonials are sore discontented, what wi' heavy taxes and injustices. He says that King Geordie may have his hands full o' rebels one day. God speed that hour!"

"What else does William say?" the boy begged eagerly.

"He speaks o' fine acres he's bought in Virginia, and how he's prosperin'. He inquires after ye. He says—" and now the keen blue eyes were searching—"He says that America is a great, bra', free land, where no man is better than his neighbor and all have equal chance. A young country for young men—an ocean removed from kings who think that they can do no wrong.

The man sighed, replaced the letter in this pocket. "Come here, laddie. Over here where I may look at ye."

Strong fingers gripped the boy's shoulders. The blue eyes probed deep. "Today I've been talkin' wi' Captain Benson, of Whitehaven, about ye," the man went on. "I know him," the boy cried. "He commands the merchant vessel *Friendship*, in the American trade."

"Ye take the words right off my tongue. It seems the Captain has had an eye on ye for some time. He thinks, mayhap, ye've the makin's of a deep-sea sailor. What say ye, laddie? Should ye like to sail wi' Benson, as apprentice?"

Over the sudden thickness in his throat, John Paul stammered, "You—do you mean it, Uncle?"

The other nodded, eyes twinkling.

The boy drew a deep breath. "There's nothing in the world I'd rather do!" he managed.

"I had an idea 'twas so. I've already signed the papers. Ye sail a week hence. But—" and the man's voice grew stern— "mark what I'm sayin'. 'Tis a hard life before the mast. Full o' danger and small reward. America's on the other side of that far sea, and there ye may make yer way, even as William has done. But if all should go wrong, have ye the character to stand fast and see it through? Or will ye come slinkin' home to Solway Firth and say, 'Uncle, I made a mistake. There's no place for me in the big world. Here's where I belong.' Is that what ye'll be sayin'?"

"I thought you knew me better than that."

"Hoots! 'Tis only jokin' I am, laddie, to keep my courage up to let ye go. The cottage will be sore lonely. But whatever befalls ye in America, hold the memory o' Culloden in yer heart. Who knows? God may one day grant ye the honor o' striking a blow for the brave lads—yer ain clansmen—who fell to Cumberland's men on that bloody ground."

The words seemed to fill the room like a prophecy and a challenge. And suddenly the cottage was too small to hold John Paul. The walls of it pressed in upon him and he couldn't breathe. He flung open the door, stumbled into the outer darkness. Rain stung his cheeks like hail. The wind's moan was the skirling of bagpipes. Black clouds billowed against the sky, like the barren hills of Culloden. But somewhere off beyond the storm and darkness—stranger than legend, brighter than a dream—a great continent lay waiting. Waiting for him. America.

The boy shut his eyes tight and there was a taste of salt upon his lips. He flung up his head. "Almighty God," he whispered. "I thank thee."

⇥⇢⇉⇒◉◈◉⇐⇇⇠⇤

Yes, perhaps the answer to the riddle of John Paul Jones lay in his childhood—in that night when a chill wind stalked the shores of Solway Firth, and an old man spoke, in bitterness, of Culloden.

CHAPTER TWO

A MAN NAMED JONES

The brigantine *Betsy* lay at anchor in the harbor of Tobago, British West Indies. In the after-cabin a slim, wide-shouldered young man, tanned by sun and wind, opened the logbook at a fresh page. He dipped a quill in ink, then hesitated, while his troubled gaze went wandering through the cabin window. On shore, he could see the English settlers' white houses shimmering in the heat. From the flagstaff at Government House the British Union Jack flapped idly. To the west, the Spanish island called Trinidad lay like a cloud-shadow on the horizon.

Stern View of the Royal William Firing a Salute, by Peter Monamy, a British painter (1681–1749).

Captain Paul's glance returned to the logbook. With determined strokes he wrote, "April 13, 1773. Crew unpaid for six months. Situation grave. First Mate Hollis is inciting the men to mutiny . . ."

John Paul's lips tightened. He was confident that he had driven a shrewd bargain for the island's first crop of sugar. It would fetch a fine profit in London. There the crew would be paid off, with a handsome bonus to boot. But the purchase had left the young Captain without immediate funds. The ugly temper of the crew could no longer be disregarded. With the second officer ill in his bunk, and Mr. Hollis encouraging the men to rebelling, was ever a captain more sorely beset? And so John Paul's eyes were troubled as he penned the fateful word *mutiny*.

For a second his mind cast back over the thirteen years that had passed since leaving the cottage on the shores of Solway Firth. What crowded years they had been! His service under Captain Benson had laid the foundations of seamanship that were to serve him so well through all his later years. From apprentice he had risen swiftly to foremast hand; from bosun to mate; finally to sailing-master. With his brother William, in Virginia, he had discovered no common bond save the family name. William was wedded to his acres, to his crops and cattle, while John Paul was just as surely marked for a life at sea. Though the older brother had urged the boy to remain ashore, the sea beckoned and could not long be denied. At nineteen, young John Paul, already a qualified officer, had signed aboard an African slave ship—a respectable enough pursuit in those times. But the sufferings and hardships inflicted upon the human cargo had been intolerable to him. The sea never hardened John Paul to cruelty. Two years later he was again in the merchant service, this time in command of the *Betsy*.

Then came the unfortunate affair of Mungo Maxwell, a turning-point in his life. Abruptly John Paul closed the logbook and pushed back in his chair. Why should that name rise to haunt him now? He stood for a second at the cabin window, glancing forward along the decks where the crew was gathered in sullen knots of men. Mr. Hollis, lolling in the shade of the midships awning, was making no effort to spur them to their tasks.

Mungo Maxwell . . . John Paul clenched his fists. Perhaps it was Tobago that stirred that hateful, painful memory; for it was here in this very harbor, two years back, that he had ordered Maxwell, the ship's carpenter, flogged for refusal to obey orders. The punishment had been a light one for such an offense, and richly deserved. But the carpenter had lodged a complaint with the island's Chief Magistrate. The case came to trial.

John Paul was freed from blame by the courts. Maxwell, transferring to another ship, died some months later of a fever contracted in Africa.

But in Tobago, where the *Betsy's* young Captain counted enemies among his rivals, ugly rumors began to spread— rumors that crept from island to island, even finding their way across the sea to England. It was whispered that Mungo

Maxwell had died of the flogging received at the hands of John Paul. Even though the courts had declared the young Captain blameless, wherever he went John Paul found himself trailed by a scandal that had no justification in fact. For him the bright island called Tobago was filled with shadows. Once the cargo of sugar was aboard, he'd weigh the *Betsy's* anchor and be rid of the place forever!

The door banged open and a man stepped into the cabin. John Paul swung around to confront his first mate. The insolent leer on Hollis's face told him at once that matters had come to a head.

"You see fit to dispense with the ceremony of knocking, Mister?" the Captain demanded coldly.

The mate slouched against the door. His pale, close-set eyes shifted. "Nobody in this ship is standin' on ceremony any longer," he snapped.

John Paul stiffened. "And what do you mean by that, sir?"

"I mean that the men are touchy as gunpowder," the other retorted. "Something's got to be done about it, and right now."

Captain surveyed the man who stood so defiantly before him. He didn't like what he saw. The shifty glance, the pock-marked skin that even a tropical sun seemed powerless to color, belonged more to a jail-bird than to a seaman. "And what have you been doing about it, Mister?" he demanded.

Hollis's eyes narrowed. "I've been passin' along your promises," he shot back. "But the men won't be put off longer with easy words. Six months now without a cent of wages! No clothes to their backs but the rags they shipped in."

"If it's clothing that troubles them," the other returned, "I'll have every man outfitted at my own expense from the ship's stores."

"Tah!" the mate exploded scornfully. "They're used to wearin' rags. It's spendin'-money and shore leave what's on their mind."

John Paul fought down a rising tide of anger. "Mister, perhaps you are aware that I stand within my legal rights in withholding the men's wages until the cargo is sold. They will be paid off in London, with a five-pound bonus for every man."

"Legal rights be blasted!" The mate's lips drew back from his teeth. "We want our money now and we'll have it—or know the reason why."

"Ah! So you throw in your own grievance with the men, Mr. Hollis? A first officer who becomes a mouthpiece for insubordination is new to my experience." John Paul's voice hardened, his eyes flashed. "I've put up with a goodly bit from you, Mister. You have shirked your duties abominably, sir, and sided with the men against their Captain. Now get this into your head: if there's more of it in future, I shall remove you from duty and see that you get your deserts when we return to England."

Beside himself, the mate shouted, "Go ahead, then! Remove me from duty. My word will carry as much weight with the owners as yours—any day."

"You'll answer in court for this, Hollis."

"Court, is it?" the other flung back. "You may do a bit of answerin' yourself, Johnny Paul. Mungo Maxwell's dead, *but his name ain't!* Not by a long sea-mile. You flogged him to death, and every man-Jack in this ship knows it."

White to the lips, John Paul swept his sword from its scabbard. Before the relentless blaze of his eyes the mate recoiled, backed toward the door.

"I—I didn't mean that," Hollis stammered, his voice changing to half a whine. "It's only what the men have been sayin'—" Hurriedly he twisted the latch and flung open the door.

In that second a chorus of angry voices assailed the Captain's ear. The mate stepped nimbly beyond harm's reach. With shoulders squared and sword in hand John Paul braced himself to meet the band of men who moved as a solid block toward him. Some were armed with cutlasses, others with clubs. In the lead a bearded ruffian named Blackton clutched a short, ugly dagger in one fist.

"Stand where you are!" cried John Paul; and something in that commanding voice, so accustomed to obedience, brought the mutineers to an uncertain pause.

The lean, whip-strong body that faced them so fearlessly filled the men with momentary dismay. They looked to Blackton, their leader, for support.

"What is the meaning of this?" thundered the Captain. "You, Blackton, speak up and quick about it!"

"It means we've had aplenty of this-here ship," the sailor shouted back, brandishing the dagger. "And enough of a skinflint skipper, too. We know our rights. Where's our wages?"

"Aye," echoed a dozen growling voices. "We'll have our pay or know why. And shore leave, what's more."

"You'll be paid when we reach England," the Captain answered, controlling himself with effort. "In addition, there'll be five pounds for every man."

"You've put us off for the last time, John Paul," snarled Blackton. "We're takin' no more promises, and no more orders from the likes o' you."

"You can be hanged for this, Blackton, and well you know it."

"Hangin', is it?" the other taunted. "Maybe you'll be the one that swings from the *Betsy*'s yardarm—if we don't heave you overside first for shark-bait."

John Paul raked the crew with his glance. "Back to your stations, men," he commanded. "Don't listen to this fool! You all know the penalty for mutiny. Every man of you will swing for it."

Involuntarily the men paused, eyeing one another. They knew the truth of the Captain's assertion. That fearless figure, with his back to the cabin door and sword in hand, filled them with uncertainty. Blackton had led them into this. It was up to him to prove that he was capable of being their leader. Mr. Hollis, the sneer again on his lips, stood well to one side, watching to see which way the tide of mutiny might turn.

Sensing the indecision of his followers, Blackton flung a shout over his shoulder. "Up and at him, mates! Now's your chance!"

John Paul braced himself. "For the last time, men," he called, "I warn you—"

"Save your gab for the sharks," snarled Blackton. He gripped the dagger at right angles to his stomach and crouched forward. For him no retreat was possible. He could only advance.

The dam of John Paul's rage burst. He swung his sword like a blade of light. Before that relentless movement Blackton made the error of stepping back, thus giving the now thoroughly aroused Captain room to attack. A second sweep of the sword caught the sailor's knife and sent it spinning into the scuppers. For a split-second the mutineer, unarmed and at the Captain's mercy, paused. Then he wheeled, broke and ran. His followers, dismayed at their leader's action, parted as if by magic to let him escape. Through their broken ranks John Paul dashed in pursuit of the scoundrel who had defied his authority and threatened his life.

Forward along the decks the two men raced, a scant ten feet apart. Behind them moved the crew, whose will to revolt had strangely collapsed. Mr. Hollis hovered to one side, his face stamped with fear.

At the mainmast Blackton drew up short. He seized an iron belaying pin from the fife rail. Then, like a rodent brought to bay, he swung to face his pursuer. By its own impetus the Captain's body struck his enemy's in head-on collision. Both men staggered, reeled apart.

For the space of a second they paused, eyeing each other, breathing hard. Taller than John Paul, with a longer reach,

Blackton was a tough opponent. The belaying pin, one blow of which could crush a skull, glittered in the sunlight. The crew watched in breathless silence. Death hung by a thread.

Then with a furious oath Blackton charged in. The belaying pin swung wildly. John Paul ducked under the sweep of the iron bar. A cold rage filled him now. This towering ruffian meant to kill him. It was unbelievable, but there it was. No quarter would be asked or given. There could be but one end: his own life or Blackton's. Again the mutineer lunged. But the weight of the bar swung his body off balance. Instantly John Paul stepped in. The point of the sword struck his enemy's right side and drove deep between the ribs.

With a shrill, choking cry the mutineer lurched to his knees. The belaying pin hit the deck with a ringing ping. Blackton's hands clutched at his ribs, as if to hold back the tide of his life's blood. A second more and he plunged face-forward. His body twitched, lay still. From around him the mutineers drew back, glancing dazedly from the lifeless figure to the white-lipped man who stood above it.

"Blackton's dead . . ." The whisper ran through the crowd on a note of unbelief. The men seemed powerless to move, as if a spell had been fixed upon them. Even Mr. Hollis had been struck dumb by the turn of events. The mutiny which he had planned with such cunning had collapsed like a pricked bubble. Without a leader, the men were so many sheep.

John Paul cast aside the stained sword. Above the sickness in his heart he faced the first mate. "Mr. Hollis," he said, finding his voice, "I am going ashore at once to present my

JOBS ABOARD SHIP

BOSUN (BOATSWAIN):
Usually one of the best sailors, he was in charge of all deck activities such as dropping the anchor and handling the sails. He issued orders with a silver boatswain's whistle.

FOREMAST HAND:
The foremast is the mast most forward, or nearest the bow, on the ship. Hands are members of the ship's crew. To hand a sail is to furl it.

MATE:
An officer just under the master.

QUARTERMASTER:
He steers the ship.

SAILING MASTER:
The officer charged with the sailing of the ship.

ON A MAN-OF-WAR

COX (COXSWAIN):
He has charge of the boat and crew in the absence of officers. On a man-of-war, he had charge of the Captain's boat.

POWDER BOYS OR MONKEYS:
These boys collected bags of gunpowder or powder cartridges from the magazine and carried them to the guns.

MARINE:
Marines were not sailors; they were soldiers who served aboard a man-of-war. They served as sharpshooters, in gun crews, with boarding parties, and as sentries.

case to the Magistrate. You, as first officer, will accompany me. You will testify to the fact that these men have mutinied, that I was forced to kill their leader in defense of my life."

The mate rallied. His lips twitched. "I've taken the last of your orders," he jeered. "I'll testify before the Magistrate, all right, but it won't be the way you want. You've played right into my hands, Johnny Paul. The *Betsy*'s mine now, and her cargo will be split in equal shares with every man aboard." He swung toward the crew, a wild light of triumph in his eyes. "How about it, mates," he shouted. "Did you ever refuse to obey the Captain's orders?"

The men responded to the drift of the wind. Fifteen voices shouted back as one. "Not us! Who's to prove it?"

"Didn't you see the Captain strike down your ship-mate in cold blood?" Hollis demanded.

"Aye, that we did," came the answering shout, as new confidence seeped back into the wretched souls. "Poor Blackton, as wouldn't hurt a fly. Murdered in cold blood he was. *We'll* testify, all right."

Hollis turned toward the Captain, and in his eyes gleamed the hard, dangerous soul of the man. "There's your answer, Johnny Paul," he gloated. "*Now* take your story to the Magistrate and see what he makes of it."

Silently the young Captain stared around at the circle of faces so stamped with hatred and defiance. He picked up his sword, wiped the blade and slipped it into the scabbard. The men fell back, hushed now, as he strode toward the bulwarks where a rope ladder descended into a dinghy. Not a hand or a voice was raised against him. The distant beach shimmered in the heat. From the flagstaff at Government House the Union Jack flapped idly.

John Paul dropped into the dinghy. He seized the oars and pointed the bow of his craft shoreward. There was a terrible numbness in the region of his heart.

Sir Geoffrey Hamilton, Chief Magistrate of Tobago, listened gravely to the young man who sat on the other side of the long table. Flies droned in the breathless air.

"And that, sir, is the full story," John Paul concluded. "Every word is the truth. I fought in defense of my life. I am ready to stand trial—but I insist that it be a fair one. Those mutineers must be brought to justice. My name shall be cleared of all blame!"

For a long moment the Magistrate was silent, having no heart for the business at hand. "I believe in you," Sir Geoffrey said at last. "But you must remember that this is the second time within two years that you have been charged with a death by violence in Tobago. Your enemies have kept the name of Mungo Maxwell alive. Whatever your justification in *this* case, the whole island will be aroused against you."

"Surely," John Paul protested hotly, "the Governor-General will hear the evidence. Am I to be condemned unheard, sir?"

Sir Geoffrey brushed aside the words. "The Governor is a cautious old duffer," he replied, "answerable only to the King. Believe me, he'll drop your case like a red-hot chestnut."

John Paul stared back to the other in disbelief. "Is it possible," he demanded, "that an Admiralty Court would set the word of a pack of mutineers above that of a ship's commander?"

"There will be the testimony of fifteen men and your own first officer against you," the Magistrate reminded him. "You haven't a single witness to speak in your defense. Would God that unfortunate Maxwell affair had never occurred."

"But my innocence was established in court," John Paul protested.

"I know, I know. But there are those who refuse to accept the court's verdict." Sir Geoffrey shook his head. "By nightfall Tobago will be too hot to hold you, John Paul. Nor should you risk returning to England." His eyes searched the other's face. "Take my advice for what it's worth: leave this island at once! 'Tis utter madness to remain. Write off the *Betsy* and her cargo as a poor bargain. I'll see that you're safely carried to Trinidad. You'll be safer in Spanish hands than British. When a ship leaves Port-o'-Spain for Virginia, take it! There's always room for a man like you in America, John Paul. That's a big country. What happened here today won't matter there tomorrow." The Magistrate arose, extended his hand. "Forget this whole miserable affair if you can," he begged. "Make a new start for yourself—with a fresh name."

The once proud figure of John Paul drooped. To think that all his years of struggle, of high hope, should have come to such a sorry end. He recognized the wisdom of Sir Geoffrey's advice, but it was unbearable to one of his nature to run away. Yet what other choice had he? Too clearly he understood it. If he remained in Tobago, his enemies would see him swing like a criminal from the gallows or—even worse—rot out the remainder of his days in some foul jail.

He stiffened with decision. With level eyes he stared at the Englishman who waited too anxiously for his reply. "It appears that I have no choice but to accept your advice," he said quietly. "I shall start life over again in America. As for a fresh name—what name would you suggest?"

"Something that men forget easily," the other answered. "Smith, perhaps. Or Brown . . ."

A bitter smile twisted John Paul's lips. "Let it be *Jones*!" he shot back. "Who could remember a name like John Paul Jones? God willing, he shall never trouble you again, sir."

The two men gripped hands. Sir Geoffrey said, "I shall give orders at once to place a cutter at your disposal. God speed you, lad. May the New World bring you better fortune."

Without reply the young man strode swiftly across the room, through the doorway and down the steps of the wide veranda. In the harbor the *Betsy* still rode at anchor, her hull white against the glittering blue Caribbean. On the horizon, scarcely more than a cloud, lay the haven men called Trinidad. Beyond Trinidad—what?

John Paul Jones drew a deep ragged breath. And across the years, unbidden, he seemed to hear again his uncle's voice, saying, "But if all should go wrong, have ye the character to stand fast and see it through? . . ." His fists knotted.

Perhaps it was the sunlight that blinded his eyes.

War schooners at rest in Massachusetts, 1900.

CHAPTER THREE

THE FIGHT BEGINS

As the year of 1775 drew to a close, events in the American Colonies were rushing toward a climax. A crash was coming and everyone could see it. There were men who welcomed that crash and others who dreaded it. American independence, or loyalty to the Crown? That was the problem. With Boston already pinned down by British bayonets, the North was thoroughly aroused. In the South, too, feeling ran high. For the first time the harassed Colonies, like sheep in a storm, were huddling together for their own protection. A new nation was being forged. From the pulpit of a church in Virginia, where a political meeting was being held, a lanky red-headed fellow named Patrick Henry raised a cry that roared like a wind across the land:

John Paul Jones.

"Is life so dear or peace so sweet as to be purchased at the price of chains or slavery? Forbid it, Almighty God! I know not what course others may take; but as for me, give me liberty or give me death!"

On the wings of that cry, men who were strangers to one another appeared out of nowhere. Some were eager to lend support to the Colonists; others were bent on selfish gain. In either case, there was no time to inquire into the background of any man willing to bear arms. He who would strike a blow for liberty could call himself whatever he pleased—Smith or Brown or Jones—and no questions would be asked.

Possibly for this reason when a certain stranger appeared in Virginia a year or two earlier, claiming to be the brother of William Paul, no one gave the matter a second thought. But William Paul was dead. The stranger found himself penniless, friendless and alone in a country seething with rebellion.

During the twenty months which followed, little is known of what happened to the man who now called himself John P. Jones. There can be no doubt, however, that those months of masquerading behind a name not his own were bitter gall to one of John Paul's proud spirit. To live like any evil-doer, skulking from one hiding place to another, was intolerable. He firmly intended to return one day to Tobago and clear his name for all time. But though he knew himself to be legally guiltless, the fact that he was responsible for the death of another man lay upon him like a blight. There were dark hours when John Paul lost belief in himself, when he despised of ever standing innocent in the sight of his fellows. There were months of poverty, of hunger even, when he turned his hand to whatever task might offer a crust of bread. A weaker man would have been destroyed by such an ordeal; but in John Paul Jones, unsuspected until a crisis called it forth, there was a core of steel—the hallmark of a great man.

During this period of confusion, he overlooked one priceless asset: a gift for friendship. Men of fine caliber were attracted to the level-eyed stranger whose speech had not yet lost the Scottish burr of his childhood. One such man was Joseph Hewes of Edenton, North Carolina. This particular friendship was shortly to alter the course of John Paul Jones's life.

It was the sea that brought the two men together. Owner of a prosperous shipping business, Joseph Hewes was an able judge of seamen. He recognized in the young Captain a man who knew more than most about nautical matters, and promptly engaged him for a trial voyage along the coast.

But with his new-found friend, John Paul refused to sail under false colors. He unburdened himself of the weight upon his spirit; and when he had finished the tale of his misfortune, the older man offered sound advice.

"Forget the whole matter," Hewes said, "until such time as you may clear your name. America is at war, declared or not. Soon every port will be blockaded. Returning to Tobago at this time is out of the question. Besides, have you the funds?"

For answer the young man spread empty hands.

"That settles it," the other decided. "No matter how just the cause, none but a fool enters a courthouse with an empty purse. Besides, a man of your abilities can be of great service to this country in its time of trial."

John Paul's interest quickened. "In what way, sir?" he demanded.

"General Washington," said Hewes, "is crying for ships to waylay the reinforcements being brought to the British. We have few vessels, alas, capable of engaging the enemy. Ships must be built, and there must be men to man them— men who understand the tactics of naval warfare."

"You forget, sir," John Paul reminded his friend, "that I am not an American. I am a subject of the English King."

"We are *all* subjects of the King," Hewes retorted grimly, "though we may soon change that state of affairs. But tell me—where lie your sympathies, man? Tell me true and I shall know it for the truth. Do you believe in the cause of freedom? Or is your first loyalty to the Crown?"

John Paul Jones's eyes flashed. "I owe no loyalty to the Crown," he cried, and his voice held a note of harshness. "It was the King's men who struck down my own clansmen at Culloden and left the Highlands a wasteland. It is the King's representatives in Tobago who offer me no chance to erase the blot on my name. Do you still ask me, sir, where lie my sympathies? I should count it an honor to fight for America. To die—if need be!"

Joseph Hewes placed both hands on his friend's shoulders. "Would God this country had a thousand men like you, John Paul Jones," he said. "I shall do my utmost to secure a command for you. The Continental Congress sits in Philadelphia, debating the wisdom of building ships. I am a member of the Marine Committee. We shall go to Philadelphia together, you and I, and see what can be done."

With a sense of profound gratitude in his heart, John Paul felt that his months of wandering were at an end.

Philadelphia was little more than a village sprawling on the banks of the Delaware. Few of its principal streets were cobbled. Independence Hall, where the Congress had gathered, towered above the two-story brick dwellings. The year 1775 found the city filled with marching men in all sorts of makeshift uniforms—men blazing to resist the threatened liberties of their country. But it was a city also of confusion and cross-purposes.

When Joseph Hewes arrived there, accompanied by his young friend, he found the Congress laboring frantically. Time was of utmost importance. Yet Hewes was dismayed at the conflict within the ranks. One faction argued furiously against the notion of outfitting warships at national expense. Such a proposal, they declared, would lead straight to bankruptcy. The opposing faction was equally certain that only by a powerful navy could the country be successfully defended. Unless enemy reinforcements could be prevented from reaching American shores, George Washington's army would be overpowered.

It seemed incredible to John Paul Jones that men of wisdom should be so blind to this simple truth. Consequently, he was overjoyed when, on October 13, Congress at last voted the purchase of two warships to intercept the enemy transports at Boston. The *Lexington* and the *Reprisal* were duly manned and equipped. By December the number of ships had been increased to thirteen, while the Marine Committee appointed one member for each of the thirteen Colonies. The time for action had come.

As Commander-in-Chief of the new-born navy, a New Englander named Esek Hopkins was chosen. Below him in rank were four captains and a group of first, second and third lieutenants. But the struggle over these appointments resolved itself into a bitter battle between North and South. The New Englanders insisted that the Southerners (with Washington and his generals) had usurped the army. Well then, they said, let the navy belong to the North. They had their own list of officers all drawn up, most of whom were relatives of Esek Hopkins.

At this point Joseph Hewes, ever a determined man, set his jaw and stated that North Carolina must have at least one officer on the list. The debate grew hot and angry. But stubbornly Hewes held out for an appointment of his own

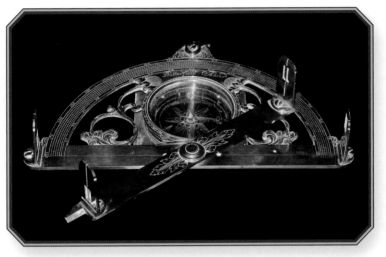

Semi-circumferentor compass.

choosing. At last it was agreed that he should be permitted to name the ranking first lieutenant.

Thus, when the first roster of the officers of the young Continental Navy appeared on December 22, 1775, it bore the name of Lieutenant John P. Jones, of North Carolina.

No one had ever heard of the man.

With Commodore Hopkins still in Providence, the task of arming and manning the flagship *Alfred* fell to Lieutenant Jones. Moored off the foot of Walnut Street, Philadelphia, the *Alfred* proved to be a lumbering bluff-bowed merchantman, with no pretense to speed or style.

But to John Paul Jones she was the proud flagship of the fleet, and he himself First Officer, thirsting for a chance to prove his mettle.

He flung himself into the assignment with boundless enthusiasm. From dawn till wintry dark he labored. There were twenty 9-pounders to be mounted, and not a ringbolt went into the gundeck that he did not test its security. Aloft in bitter winds he checked the maze of rigging for the slightest flaw. From flying jib to spanker he went over the sails, making certain that all canvas was stout and seaworthy. No detail was beneath his notice. All his years at sea—from the moment when, a boy of eleven, he had shipped from Whitehaven as apprentice—seemed to crystallize in this moment. Eager seamen swarmed up the gangway to enlist under his command. Within one week Lieutenant Jones had signed his crew. And his burning zeal so communicated itself to the men that by January, when Commodore Hopkins and Captain Saltonstall were due to arrive in the city, all was in readiness.

Three other vessels of the new fleet had likewise been set in order: the *Columbus*, a full-rigged ship of twenty guns; the *Andrew Doria* and the *Cabot*. Swinging at anchor toward the New Jersey shore of the ice-flecked river, they were joined shortly by the schooner *Hornet*. The fleet was slight in force, its equipment meager; most of the sailors had but little experience in naval warfare, the officers scarcely more. Compared to the huge and splendid royal

Navy, the Colonial squadron was indeed a trifle. But it was a beginning.

———◦◦❦◦◦———

Despite the wintry blasts from the Delaware, an immense crowd had gathered that day at the foot of Walnut Street; for news had just reached Philadelphia that the British had set fire to Norfolk and the city lay in ashes. Rumor spread that Commodore Hopkins had been ordered to proceed at once to Chesapeake Bay to attack Lord Dunmore's fleet. Men and women flocked in from the surrounding countryside, aware of the urgency of this occasion. The music of fifes and drums filled the air. The windows of the brick dwellings along the waterfront were jammed with people, waving, shouting, crying, wishing Godspeed.

On the quarterdeck of the *Alfred*, John Paul Jones paced impatiently. His clear-cut profile was well set off by a tricorn hat. He wore the full-dress uniform of the American naval officer: blue coat of the approved cut, with red lapels and slashed cuffs trimmed with gold. Above a white stock his neck rose corded and brown and strong. From his trim waist a newly acquired sword swung against his blue knee-breeches and white silk stockings. No officer of His Majesty's Royal Navy could have looked more to the quarterdeck born.

He cast a rapid eye over this ship, taking pride in each fine detail. Every man from second officer to lowliest gunner had his orders: As soon as the coach bearing the

Commodore and the Captain arrived at the pier, the 9-pounders were to sound a thirteen-gun salute—the same as that accorded to a British Admiral.

The quartermaster, in starched white ducks and tarry pigtail, was scanning the shore through a spyglass. Presently he barked, "Coach and four makin' for the pier now, sir."

Lieutenant Jones stiffened to action. His voice rang out, "All hands to quarters."

On shore, Commodore Hopkins and Captain Dudley Saltonstall stepped into a waiting barge, while the sailors saluted smartly with vertical oars.

John Paul Jones nodded to his second officer. "Lieutenant Seabury, commence firing!"

At once a glowing match was applied to the touchhole of the forward 9-pounder. With a thunderous bellow the gun shot back in its breechings. Black smoke belched forth. The fumes of sulphur and saltpeter stung the nostrils of the gunners. One after another the big guns roared out while, at the head of the gangway, the seamen stood at attention and the bosun's pipes quavered. As the last shrill note eluded, Commodore Hopkins stepped on deck.

Lieutenant Jones moved forward to greet his superior. "Honored to receive you, sir, aboard your flagship," he said; and then, scarcely turning his head, he cried, "Quartermaster, clear away the signal halyards to the maintruck."

"Aye, aye, sir!"

The halyards were quickly loosed from the belaying pins at the foot of the mainmast. Removing his hat, John

Paul Jones himself hoisted the flag. The thunder of the guns died in silence as every eye swung aloft. There a rectangle of cloth whipped bravely at the masthead—not the banner with thirteen stripes, but an ensign of yellow silk bearing a coiled rattlesnake and the motto "Don't Tread on Me."

A blood-tingling cry broke from those who watched on shore, answered by the sailors who lined the decks and clung to the rigging of the other ships. John Paul Jones was outwardly composed; no one would have guessed how deeply stirred was the young lieutenant. His hand had hoisted the first flag to be flown by the American Navy.

This was the proudest moment of his life.

Commodore Hopkins's instructions from Congress were a tall order. He was to sail at once to Chesapeake Bay and sink Lord Dunmore's fleet; then, cruising along the coast, he was to knock out any blockading frigates. After this he was to bear southeast to the West Indies and there capture all military supplies. Having completed these formidable assignments, he was instructed to proceed northward to Rhode Island, to attack and destroy any enemy forces in that region. In short, with his five converted merchant ships Esek Hopkins was expected to wipe out the entire British navy!

Unfortunately, the Commodore's only knowledge of seafaring had been gained as a brigadier-general in the land militia. Subsequent events proved him to be one of the most incompetent officers in the history of naval warfare. This fact, however, had still to be demonstrated, though it was soon only too clear to John Paul Jones. Gloomily the young lieutenant pondered the fate of the new-born navy under the leadership of such an ill-chosen man. Nor was his confidence restored by Dudley Saltonstall. Both Commodore and Captain were landsmen who, in positions of command at sea, found themselves sadly out of their depth.

All hands understood the gravity of the situation. Lord Dummore's flagship alone—the *Fowey*—outmatched any vessel in Hopkins's squadron. What chance would converted merchantmen have against the enemy's crack ships-of-the-line? Moreover, George III had promised that all rebels taken in arms at sea would be hanged as pirates. Yes, for better or worse the Colonials had committed themselves to war. There could be no turning back now.

When the *Alfred* and her consorts at last broke through the ice of the Delaware, John Paul was astonished to discover that a course had been laid not for Chesapeake Bay, but for the Bahama Islands. The shortage of gunpowder being acute in the Colonies, it was Esek Hopkins's plan first to capture the enemy's stores at Fort Montague in New Providence before proceeding to attack the English fleet. The scheme was sound enough—if it should succeed.

⚜

Running before a fresh gale, the flagship and her convoys cleared the capes of Delaware and stood on for Hatteras, that most dangerous point on the Atlantic seaboard. Lieutenant Jones quickly discovered the *Alfred* to be a "crank" vessel; she wallowed heavily, and yawed so in the following seas that two helmsmen were needed to hold the bucking wheel. The *Columbus*, the *Andrew Doria* and the *Cabot*, being square-rigged, were making out well enough with a following wind; but the schooner-rigged *Hornet* was staggering under the punishing seas. John Paul Jones stared aft at the little sloop, filled with concern lest she jibe unexpectedly and snap off her masts. He wondered if Captain Saltonstall, standing nearby on the quarterdeck, shared his own concern. But he dared not ask. Already he had discovered the Captain to be a touchy man who seemed to resent the first lieutenant.

"I could wish this devilish wind would moderate," Saltonstall muttered, shutting his spyglass with a snap. "The *Hornet*'s making a rough time of it."

"She's bound to, sir, with a wind dead aft," Jones answered. He hesitated before adding, "If the Commodore would lay a more easterly course the gale would be on our larboard quarter. That would ease the pressure mightily on the sloop, sir."

Saltonstall stared back at his first officer. His voice was icy as he said, "The Commodore needs no lessons in seamanship from you, Lieutenant Jones. Nor do I. Watch your course, sir!" With that the Captain stomped below, leaving his junior officer hot with resentment and filled with foreboding.

During the night the *Hornet* disappeared, nor was she seen again on that cruise.

FULL-RIGGED SHIP

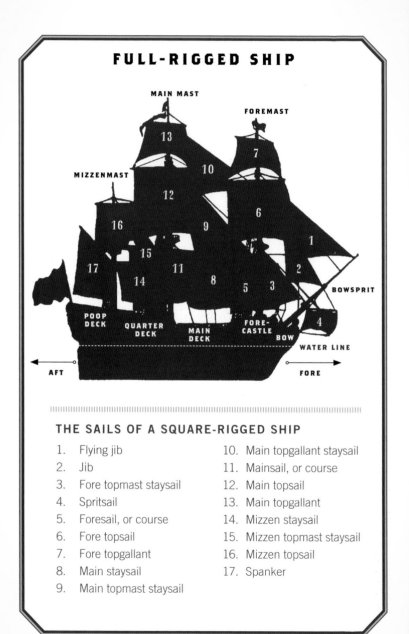

MAIN MAST

FOREMAST

MIZZENMAST

13

7

10

12

16

9

6

1

15

17

11

14

8

5

3

2

BOWSPRIT

POOP DECK

QUARTER DECK

MAIN DECK

FORE-CASTLE

BOW

4

WATER LINE

AFT

FORE

THE SAILS OF A SQUARE-RIGGED SHIP

1. Flying jib
2. Jib
3. Fore topmast staysail
4. Spritsail
5. Foresail, or course
6. Fore topsail
7. Fore topgallant
8. Main staysail
9. Main topmast staysail
10. Main topgallant staysail
11. Mainsail, or course
12. Main topsail
13. Main topgallant
14. Mizzen staysail
15. Mizzen topmast staysail
16. Mizzen topsail
17. Spanker

Dawn broke in a leaden sky. The four remaining ships, reduced to storm canvas, staggered across an ocean streaked with foam. But the stormy Cape was weathered at last. The little squadron had escaped the perils of a lee shore. A course was now laid due southeast.

Grim winter dropped slowly astern. Fairer breezes set men's spirits lifting. And when, as the fleet stood on toward the Bahama side of the Florida Straits, two British schooners were sighted in the offing, a cheer burst from the Americans. Here was luck! Prizes at last!

At once a round of shot went whistling across the Britishers' bows. They hove to immediately and were captured without further ado. Never were shipmasters more bewildered than the two English captains who had been brought up in the belief that Britannia ruled the waves. The Englishmen were brought aboard the *Alfred* for questioning. One of them, a Captain Tennant, informed Esek Hopkins that Fort Montague was heavily armed and well supplied with powder, but the garrison itself was weak. The big guns could easily beat off an attack by sea, but the fort would be vulnerable to land assault.

"Guns and powder," Hopkins gloated. "The crying need of Washington's army. They're as good as in our hands."

But this optimism found no echo in the mind of John Paul Jones. In fact, he was dismayed by the Commodore's stupidity in announcing to the enemy, by broad daylight, the arrival of the Colonial fleet. Why hadn't he held off until evening, when the ships could have slipped undetected into

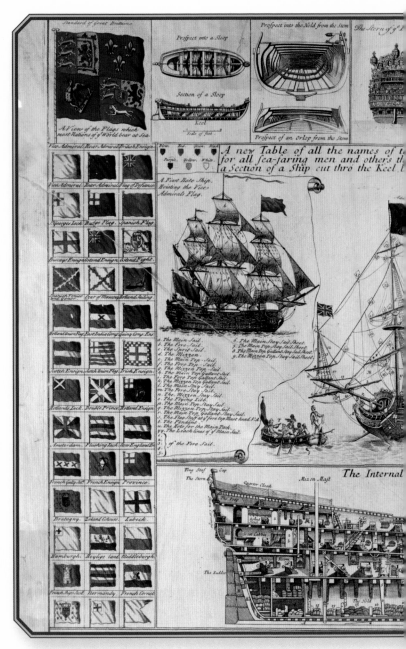

A table of all the names of the principal parts and rigging of a man-of-war.

...mpleat Model   Prospect into the hold from the Stern   Another Model

Prospect of an Orlop from the Stern

...s and Rigging of a **MAN** of **WAR** Necessary
...there with acquainted, Also all the Prospects of
...with her Boats, Longboats and Sloops.

To
the Right Hon.ble
S.r CHARLES WAGER
First Lord Comiss.r
of the Admiralty
&c.&c. this Plate is
most humbly
Inscribed.

Printed & sold by
John Bowles at N.º 13
in Cornhill, and
Carrington Bowles
at N.º 69 in St Pauls
Church Yard.

Green Flag

...carrying 96 Gunns haveing her
...her open

Fore Mast   Bowsprit

...e Stern head

The Stern

Provence	Callais	Flanders
Ter Veer	Turk	Turkish Galley
Moors	Algier	Grand Signior
Marseilles Ens.n	Piccardy	Swedes Man of War
Swedes Merch.t	Munick	Dantzick Ensign
Bremen	Rostock	Genoa Ensign
Malta	Jerusalem	Yahen
Danes Man of War	Danes Merch.t	Lunenburgh
Great.r Mogul	Bengale.r Mogul	Enchuysen
Legorne	Venice	Popes Colours
Savoy	Portugal Man of War	Portugal Merch.t
Portugal Merch.t	Amoy China	Zanguin in China
Anchonas Ens.n	Campehen Ensign	Tunis
Tripoly	Algier	Algier Colours
Tituan Colours	Salley Colours	Salley
More Araba	Ancona	Monacca

the harbor? Already the islands lay in plain sight, green and fair, with surf bursting high on their coral beaches. It was a day of hot tropical sunshine, with squalls that danced up and passed away in rainbows to leeward. Surely in this clear light the lookout at Fort Montague had already discovered the presence of the American squadron! At any moment her big guns might open up and a hail of shot come whistling across the waves.

Esek Hopkins addressed his first officer. "I understand that you are familiar with these islands, Lieutenant Jones? What do you know of the western harbor?"

"There *is* no anchorage to the west," Jones answered quickly. "Our fleet would find itself stranded on a lee shore." As the Commodore's eyebrows went up in amazement, he added, "Nor is there a road into the town from the west, sir. Before the marines could reach the fort from that direction, the enemy would be organized for defense."

Never a man to think quickly in emergencies, the Commodore glanced uncertainly toward Dudley Saltonstall, looking to that individual to suggest some solution.

Since the ship had weighed anchor in the Delaware, John Paul Jones had been a thorn in the side of Saltonstall, the older man resenting the first lieutenant's superior seamanship. With heavy sarcasm the Captain said, "As a master of strategy, Lieutenant Jones, what course would you pursue? Abandon the attack and sail back to Philadelphia empty-handed?"

"Not at all, sir," came the quiet reply. "The eastern shore of this island offers good anchorage, with a road only four miles into town. Once the marines land, the fort will be ours within an hour!"

Saltonstall's face hardened. "Are you familiar with the channel into this harbor?" he demanded.

"I am not, sir," Jones answered at once. "But we have a pilot aboard who knows it well—Captain Tennant."

"The Englishman?" exclaimed the Commodore. "Tennant's our enemy! He'd pile us on the reef for sure."

John Paul Jones permitted himself to smile. "I've learned that Tennant has a wife and family," he said. "He'd like to see them once more before he dies. With your leave, sir, I shall take Tennant with me into the crosstrees. He will point out the channel. With me at his side I guarantee there'll be no treachery on his part!"

A heated argument followed between the Commodore and the Captain. The former was for backing the plan at once, while the latter called such a decision suicidal.

In the end, the Commodore's will prevailed. "It is agreed, Lieutenant Jones," he said irritably. "But if aught goes wrong, you will pay for the mistake with a court-martial."

"Understood, sir," came the confident answer.

Orders were given to bring the fleet about at once. Within an hour the eastern end of the island had been cleared, and presently the ships found themselves off a low-lying cay fringed with reefs and dangerous shoals. To the north stretched an unbroken line of surf whose thunder resounded in the air. With leadsmen stationed in the fore-chains, chanting the depth, the flagship stood warily in toward the cay. The rest of the convoy trailed at cautious distance. The Commodore's gaze swung unhappily from the yawning reefs to the two men perched aloft in the crosstrees. Had he taken leave of his senses, Hopkins wondered, in trusting this untried lieutenant with the safety of the fleet? A heavy sigh escaped him. Saltonstall's mouth clamped in grim disapproval as he turned his back on the commanding officer.

Braced on the platform of the crosstrees beside Captain Tennant, John Paul Jones followed the direction of the Englishman's pointing finger. From this height the channel was clearly visible as it twisted among the sharp-toothed reefs. On both sides of the ship boiled white water, uncomfortably close, while the thunder of the surf deafened the ear. But the young lieutenant's voice rose clearly above the tumult as he directed the helmsmen on the quarterdeck. It was an anxious moment. The slightest miscalculation would send the ship to destruction.

And for a second Tennant stared in amazement at the man beside him. Neither short nor tall, handsome nor ugly, John Paul Jones might have passed unnoticed in a crowd; but when danger threatened he became a man transformed. His eyes blazed with blue fire; his jaw hardened like granite; his very stature seemed to increase as danger mounted. This was such a moment.

Suddenly, with a long smooth-rolling motion that was like flight, the ship shot safely past the reefs. She came to in placid water and dropped her anchors. A rousing cheer went up from the marines who stood assembled on deck, and that sound was as music to the young lieutenant in the crosstrees. The fire that had consumed him burned out as he watched the other three ships pick their way gingerly through the channel and come to anchor a cable's length from the *Alfred*.

There was orderly excitement as the marines, under Captain Nichols, prepared to storm the beach. Fifty sailors swelled the number of the landing force to three hundred. The ships stood with gunports agape, ready to loose their broadsides if the enemy should appear on the exposed road that led into the town. With envy in his heart John Paul Jones watched the men swarm ashore, saw the sun flash on pike and cutlass, and realized that his own part in the battle was at an end.

But no enemy appeared to challenge the invaders as they swept swiftly inland down the road that led to Fort Montague. In the gathering dusk the Americans raced into the town, only to discover that the Governor had fled his palace in panic and taken refuge in Fort Montague. The fort had been built originally to repel by land or sea the armadas of Spain. Properly defended, its thick-walled bastions presented a forbidding front. At any moment the big guns, plainly visible, might be expected to belch forth a fire of hot metal. More cautiously Captain Nichols ordered the advance of his men.

Scaling ladders were dragged up to the frowning walls. Then shouting wildly the marines swarmed up the ladders,

under the very muzzles of the guns. Atop the parapet, Captain Nichols stared in disbelief. Not a gun had been manned! A few scattered sentries were surrendering hastily. The Americans were in possession of the fort and all its arms. Down came the Union Jack on the run, while above the ramparts floated the Continental flag, proclaiming that the marines had won the first amphibious battle of their distinguished history.

Within a matter of minutes Governor Montfort Browne and two officers in charge of the fort surrendered command. They informed Captain Nichols that when the American squadron had first been sighted, they had despaired of defending the island with the slight force at their disposal.

The loot of Fort Montague was quickly transferred to the waiting ships: eighty-eight cannon, ranging in size from 9- to 36-pounders; fifteen large mortars; over eleven thousand round-shot; and twenty casks of precious powder. The guns alone would be cause for rejoicing in the hard-pressed Colonies. The first battle of the American Navy was an unqualified victory. Moreover, not a single casualty was reported.

That night, in his cabin, John Paul Jones wrote a letter to his friend and patron, Joseph Hewes. It is characteristic of him that in describing the battle he made no mention of his own contribution. These words concluded his letter:

"The Commander-in-Chief is respected thro' the fleet."

MILITARY "PIRATE"

Much of John Paul Jones's early career in the Navy, long before his more famous battles with British ships along the coast of England, was aimed at capturing supplies from both commercial ships and British military vessels to be used by the poorly equipped forces commanded by George Washington.

In an expedition against Nassau, in the Bahamas, Jones helped capture weapons and supplies while commanding the *Alfred*. The battle gained the Americans eighty-eight cannon and fifteen mortars and many other supplies, which would be used by George Washington's forces defending Boston.

While commanding the *Providence*, John Paul Jones captured sixteen British ships over a six-week period during the summer of 1776. Food, arms and gunpowder were seized during these conquests.

As captain of the *Alfred*, Jones captured several British warships while cruising along the coast of Nova Scotia during the fall of 1776. During these captures, he obtained warm winter clothing and coal intended for British forces, which instead helped sustain the Continental Army during the brutal year that followed.

CHAPTER FOUR

UP THE LADDER

In recognition of his services in the Bahamas, Lieutenant Jones was commissioned as a captain in the Colonial Navy. A step up the ladder. The promotion had an immediate effect: it removed him from Hopkins's flagship to a vessel of his own command.

At last John Paul Jones was on his own. Now it was up to him to prove that Joseph Hewes's faith had not been misplaced. He was given a small sloop-of-war called the *Providence*. With such a craft (as lean and swift as a bird of prey) Jones was certain that he could exhaust the enemy's strength far more effectively than would be possible with

Boston Harbor.

a larger ship. He could be here today and gone tomorrow—swooping, pouncing, wheeling away—a veritable hawk of the seas. And with this conviction, John Paul's old self-confidence swept through him like a tide.

The *Providence* boasted only twelve 4-pound guns, mounted on the maindeck. By comparison to a British frigate she was a mere cockleshell. But her single mast was placed well forward and smartly raked; her hull was as lean as a shark's. Besides a huge fore-and-aft mainsail she carried on trim yards a square-rigged topsail. Her array of jibs might have seemed to a landsman to be out of proportion to all wise practice; but John Paul Jones knew better. Given half a chance, his sloop-of-war would show her heels to any British frigate in the blockading fleet.

Moreover, the Naval Committee's orders pleased the young Captain mightily: He was to convoy the brig *Zephyr*, heavily laden with guns for the defense of New York, through the British squadron off Narragansett Bay. After that, he was to cruise in any direction he might choose—destroying enemy shipping or taking prizes. The loss of the *Zephyr*'s armament, however, would be a serious blow to the Colonies. The brig must be protected at all costs. In this matter Captain Jones must not fail.

―――――――――

To be at sea again, in command of his own ship, was vastly exciting to John Paul Jones. He rejoiced too in having a fine crew—sixty hands all told. Lieutenant Jared Folger, of

Nantucket, in particular pleased him. Here was an officer after John Paul Jones's own heart. The two men were destined to fight side by side through many a tight spot, until the day came when one of them would give his life in his country's *cause . . .*

The *Providence* was running free with all sail set and drawing handsomely. In admiration the Captain studied her performance as she clipped across the wind-whipped waters of Block Island Sound. The sloop was an even cleaner sailer than he had dared to hope! The brig *Zephyr*, staggering under her cargo of precious guns, was holding dogged pace astern.

Suddenly from the lookout in the crosstrees there came a shout: "Sail ho! Sail ho to wind'ard!"

"What do you make of her?" Jones bellowed.

"Full-rigged ship. Britisher, by the cut of her tops'ls—"

Glass in hand, Captain Jones swung into the ratlines. He'd been warned that His Majesty's frigate *Cerberus*, thirty-two guns, was patrolling this region of the Sound. Even as he swept the telescope to his eye his worst fears were confirmed. Under a tremendous press of canvas the heaviest British frigate on the coast was standing toward the *Providence*—a bulldog advancing relentlessly upon a terrier.

Jones's mind raced forward and back to meet the emergency. There was no chance of outfighting such a man-o'-war, any pair of whose heavy guns outmatched the entire broadside of the *Providence*. There was still ample time for the sloop to escape if she came about at once and fled northward. Such a desertion, however, would deliver the *Zephyr* and her valuable cargo into the hands of the enemy. Jones's crew was clinging to the rigging, staring in awed fascination at the mighty frigate. What would Captain Jones do? Why didn't he come about and make a dash for safety? Soon it would be too late to escape. The *Cerberus* would send them all to Davy Jones's Locker and the *Zephyr* would be captured anyway.

The Captain's answer was prompt. "Mr. Folger, turn out all hands! Set jib and mizzen stays'l."

"Aye aye, sir."

Instantly the sloop responded to the added press of canvas. She fairly leaped through the waves, foam creaming along her sides. The brig was still plodding desperately in her protector's wake.

"*Zephyr* ahoy!" bellowed Captain Jones through the trumpet. "Make all sail due west! You're on your own now. Good luck!"

The men in the brig, their faces plainly visible, were certain then that John Paul Jones was abandoning the *Zephyr* to her doom. Mr. Folger thought likewise. So did the crew. But to them all it seemed that Captain Jones had no other choice. Why lose two ships when one could be saved? Yet their hearts were heavy as they thought of Washington's guns, which now surely would fall into the hands of the enemy.

Thus Mr. Folger was taken aback to hear the Captain shout, "Hard down the helm!"

Astounded, the helmsman echoed stupidly, "Hard down, sir?" He could not believe his ears. Such a course would head the sloop not away from the advancing frigate but straight into its guns!

"Hard down is what I said," snapped Captain Jones. "Smart about it! I'll have my ship laid athwart the bows of the enemy."

The *Providence* came smartly about as the tiller went hard down. With satisfaction Jones noted that the *Zephyr* was making desperate haste to westward as his own ship wheeled to engage the mighty *Cerberus*.

Impulsive, John Paul Jones might be; but under conditions where one false move meant destruction, he was never foolhardy. Already a plan of action was clearcut in his mind. If his ruse succeeded, the *Zephyr* would escape with her cargo. If it failed—well, such were the fortunes of war. But John Paul Jones's men had yet to see their madcap skipper in action. At this moment they were certain that he meant to sacrifice their lives in hopeless contest. They didn't understand that Jones was trying to out-guess the British commander. With the *Zephyr* fleeing west into the safety of Long Island Sound, and the sloop heading in the opposite direction, to which one would the *Cerberus* give chase?

John Paul Jones chuckled to himself even as he put the question. No British commander would dare to face his officers if he permitted a sloop-of-war to escape while he ran off to pursue an unarmed merchantman!

Captain Jones's chuckle burst into a laugh. Look you, Mr. Folger—the old washtub has decided to give *us* chase. There's more than a chance now that the *Zephyr* will get through to safety. Send the hands to quarters and clear for action. Hoist the colors."

"Aye aye, sir!" came Folger's reply. His spirits had gone bounding upward.

The rattlesnake emblem streaked to the peak and fluttered wildly on the wind. The drums went roaring through the sloop, beating the men to quarters. Weeks of tiresome drill were now justified as each man sprang to his post.

"I'll have the guns loaded with two rounds of dismantling shot, if you please," barked the Captain.

"Aye aye, sir."

Sweating gun-crews slewed the 4-pounders forward to bear on the mighty frigate. The powder boys came racing, each with a coil of smoldering slow-match in a tub.

The gun-captain shouted, "Run 'em out, lads!"

The men threw their weight on the tackles and the cannon ran out. For a second John Paul Jones thought with satisfaction of the dismantling shot: lengths of wicked iron chain, joined to a single iron ring in the center. When discharged, it would hurtle like a rocket from the guns, shredding the enemy's rope and canvas.

Mr. Folger touched his hat. "Ship cleared for action, sir."

"Excellent! I'll have one bow-chaser fired, if you please."

"Aye aye, sir."

The gun barked—a single shot of cocky warning. Now the clumsy frigate was coming about. Her starboard bow-chaser bellowed angrily, but the ball fell twenty feet short of the dancing sloop. Running free, with every sheet and tack manned, the *Providence* fairly leaped over the waves as she wheeled, drawing off the enemy in pursuit. Jones was prudent enough, however, not to pull so far ahead as to discourage the British commander. Tantalizingly the sloop hovered just beyond range of the enemy's guns—now on one tack, again on another, while the frigate lost all headway as she clumsily attempted to box about in the sloop's wake. And when at last from the crosstrees it was seen that the *Zephyr* had dropped so far below the horizon as to be beyond capture, Captain Jones clapped his lieutenant's shoulder.

"The brig's safe," he exulted. "More guns for Washington's army. A ration of grog to all hands, Mr. Folger! We'll drink a toast to the Colonies: long may they wave!"

But Folger pointed doubtfully. "The frigate's coming round to try for a broadside," he warned.

"Let her," came the cheery response. "Every ball will fall short. She'll never catch us now!"

The words had barely left Captain Jones's lips when the angry *boom* of the enemy's broadside thundered across the waves.

"Ha!" crowed Jones with delight. "The bulldog salutes the terrier. Thirty-two guns! 'Pon my soul, enough for a brace of admirals. Clear the stern-chaser, Mr. Folger. Stand by to reply."

There came the single bark of the terrier's answer: cheerful effrontery.

"You may secure the battery now, Mr. Folger."

"Aye aye, sir," came the happy answer. "And three hurrahs for Cap'n Jones's, men!"

BATTLE STRATEGY

Much like George Washington, who also faced vastly superior British fighting forces, John Paul Jones created his own strategies for fighting successfully at sea. Military historians call this kind of military strategy "asymmetrical warfare." In the case of John Paul Jones, this meant fighting in a series of unexpected hit-and-run attacks and, where direct confrontation was not avoidable, fighting in a manner that was unlike what the enemy was expecting.

Because the American Navy had not nearly enough ships to protect its own coasts, Jones, with the backing of important members of Congress and diplomats such as Benjamin Franklin, realized that hit-and-run attacks on ports on the British coast would cause the British to move its own ships back to Britain and away from the American coast in order to protect itself. Much of Jones's career was spent doing just this—quick and shocking attacks on ports and docked ships along the British coast.

In direct naval battles, Jones always made good use of the capabilities of his ships. When commanding a smaller, faster ship, he darted here and there, attacking and retreating before heavier, better-armed warships could maneuver. When commanding a heavier, slower ship, Jones's strategy was to sail into direct contact with the enemy ship, where hand-to-hand fighting could win the battle.

John Paul Jones had a reputation for being difficult to get along with, and he alienated some of the politicians and fellow naval commanders of the day. But he was truly a gifted commander when it came to fighting on the high seas.

Chart of sea coast: England, Ireland, and Scotland.

A lively cheer burst from every throat as the *Providence*, with sheets trimmed flat, hauled by the wind and raced away to safety.

———◇◆◇———

But John Paul Jones had not yet seen the last of the *Cerberus*. The British commander, smarting with shame, was determined to send the cocky sloop-of-war to the bottom of the Atlantic. He very nearly succeeded.

Two days after the first encounter, the *Providence* was again cruising warily off Block Island when the lookout sighted a heavily laden brigantine coming up over the horizon. Immediately Captain Jones set out to investigate.

When close enough to answer signals, the stranger was discovered to be the *Buccaneer* out of Santo Domingo, bound for New York with a cargo of military supplies for the Colonial Army. Even as the signals were caught and answered, the headsails of a frigate were observed in the west, bearing down at full speed upon the helpless *Buccaneer*. Within minutes a roundshot from the frigate's bows splashed dangerously close under the brigantine's stern, ordering her to heave to at once.

"The *Cerberus* again," muttered Mr. Folger. "I'd recognize those tops'ls if I saw 'em in Zanzibar! She means business this time, sir."

"Aye," agreed Jones calmly. "We'll not disappoint her. But let us remember she has a score to even. Beat to quarters, Mr. Folger."

Once again the roll of drums sounded through the sloop, calling the hands to battle stations.

From the poop, Captain Jones addressed his crew. "Men," he cried, "we have the honor of engaging His Majesty's *Cerberus*. We outwitted her once. Can we do it again?"

Sixty voices shouted as one, "Aye, that we can! Up and at her! We'll trim her sails!"

By this time the frigate was close enough for the checkerboard of her open gunports to be seen, piercing the white stripe that marked her sides. Surely the British commander had already recognized the sloop-of-war! With a fat prize in the offing, would he again allow himself to be decoyed into a wild-goose chase? Captain Jones thought not. For the *Cerberus*, ignoring the sloop, was standing doggedly on toward the brigantine, whose canvas shivered helplessly, giving her the aspect of a lamb about to be devoured by a wolf.

This tactic suited John Paul Jones. Already the light of battle was dancing in his eyes—that wicked gleam his men had come to recognize and respect. Through his glass Jones could now see the white decks of the enemy, the gold lace of the officers and the red jackets of the marines on the quarterdeck.

"Stand by to come about—" he barked.

"Stand by it is, sir!"

Keeping well to windward, the sloop raced along the frigate's starboard flank, with a fine view of her ports triced open and bristling with guns. When well on the enemy's quarter, the sloop's helm went up. Instantly before the wind the *Providence* romped down to the stern of her mighty opponent, keeping too far aft for the Britisher's broadside to be brought to bear. Thus only the frigate's two stern-chasers were left to challenge the sloop's battery. The *Cerberus* was listing steeply to leeward, so that her crews were unable to train the chasers on the racing sloop.

As the *Providence* crossed the enemy's wake, John Paul Jones cried, "Aim high for the mains'l! A hole there will check her speed."

Mr. Folger bent to squint along his gun. He gave a twirl to the elevating screw and waited for a favorable wave. Then he stood aside and jerked the lanyard. The gun boomed and recoiled.

"Another one!" roared Jones.

A sponge was thrust hissing into the hot metal. A cartridge of paper was ripped open and shoved into the muzzle. Instantly a rammer packed the charge up harder, followed by a felt wad. Then the ball went rolling home. Folger gauged the motion of the ship, again jerked the lanyard. Once more the 4-pounder bellowed, leaped back in its breechings. Then gun after gun thundered a full broadside.

Jones clambered up on the bulwarks. And suddenly, to his vast delight, he saw the frigate's main-topsail collapse. Perhaps this was the beginning of what was later to be his formula: get the enemy's rigging first, cripple her speed, and then pound her at leisure.

"Fine shot, men!" he cried, his face aglow. "We've hit her square." His teeth flashed bare and white against a face blackened by powder-smoke. The enemy's spanker-gaff was hanging lifeless, the upper half of the sail blowing out like a shirt on a clothesline. Captain Jones grinned. Nothing like dismantling shot!

"Blast me, lads," Jared Folger was shouting excitedly, "we've clipped her wings. Clap an eye on her tops'l yard!"

The latter had come crashing down, smothering the helmsmen in canvas. At the same instant the frigate's mainsail split from clew to earing. The shouts of the British officers, the frantic cries of the men could be heard across the water.

"Up helm!" barked Jones. "We'll give her another round. On the lee quarter this time."

While the frigate sought desperately to clear her decks of canvas and rigging, the sloop came racing up under her stern from leeward, this time bringing the starboard battery to bear. Again the guns roared out. And for the second time in two days the commander of the *Cerberus* found himself in a quandary: if he gave chase to the *Buccaneer*, the Yankee sloop would continue to tack back and forth across his stern, riddling his sails with dismantling shots. Already his ship had lost steerageway. If, on the other hand, he came about to bring a broadside to bear on the *Providence*, the brigantine would surely escape, while the sloop was much too agile to be caught napping. Still, there was nothing else to be done but get rid of this pestering gadfly. The infuriated British commander snapped an order.

A cheer burst from John Paul's men as they watched the bulldog frigate come heavily about. They knew that once again Captain Jones had outwitted the enemy.

"I'll have the guns secured, Mr. Folger," Jones was saying calmly. "But don't crowd on too much sail. We're going to be chased again and I should not like to discourage His Majesty."

Folger grinned happily, wiped his sweating face. "We'll lead the old weevil-box a merry chase, sir, then walk away," he promised.

Doggedly the commander of the *Cerberus* was setting all possible canvas. He'd finish off this Yankee upstart once and for all! His men had worked miracles in sending up a new topsail yard, and John Paul Jones paid them a grudging respect as he saw sail after sail break free and swell to the breeze. Stunsails were being outrigged and doused with water, the better to hold the wind. At last the frigate got under majestic way and stood toward the tantalizing sloop. The *Buccaneer*, meanwhile, had taken to her heels and was dropping rapidly astern toward safety. The enemy's bow-chasers thundered and water spouted under the stern of the sloop, dangerously close; but before the guns could be reloaded and again brought to bear, the *Providence* was romping away on a new course.

Not until he was assured that the *Buccaneer* was indeed beyond capture, however, did Captain Jones abandon his cat-and-mouse game with the enemy.

Then it was, "Haul by the wind, Mr. Folger!" Jones wiped the spray from his eyes, and a smile broke over his taut face as his ship sped away to safety. With two 4-pounder broadsides he had outmatched a mighty frigate. How Joseph Hewes would relish the story of this encounter! And the words sang like a refrain in John Paul Jones's mind: "More guns for Washington's army."

Captain Jones was convinced that only by carrying the war into enemy territory could the Colonies hope to win recognition of their cause. If enough British shipping was destroyed, he felt confident that the merchants of London would soon be favoring American independence.

For this reason, after evading the guns of the *Cerberus* for a second time, the *Providence* set forth on a cruise that the Royal Navy was to have good reason to remember.

September was at hand—the month when the fishing fleet of Nova Scotia dried and salted their catch against the long winter months to come. A blow struck successfully in that quarter would soon make itself felt across the ocean. More important still, it would help to draw some of the blockading fleet away from the New England coast.

Within a week after sailing north, the *Providence* had taken two prizes: the *Britannia* and the *Sea Nymph*—West Indiamen laden with rum for London. They were captured without a struggle. In charge of prize crews they were dispatched at once to Philadelphia.

SHIP RANKINGS

1ST RATE
100 guns or more
3 gun decks
Line of battleships
Ship of the line (fit to lie in main
battle formation)

2ND RATE
90 to 98 guns
3 gun decks
Line of battleships
Ship of the line (fit to lie in main
battle formation)

3RD RATE
64 to 84 guns
2 gun decks
Standard fighting ship. Noted
for balance of fire-power and
maneuverability.

4TH RATE
50 to 60 guns
Below 64 guns considered too
weak to be in line

5TH RATE
28 to 40 guns
Task: cruise and destroy
Single gun deck
Frigates. Fast and powerful.
Most glamorous. Used for
scouting, protecting merchant
convoys.

6TH RATE
20 to 24 guns

UNRATED SLOOPS
8 to 12 guns
Cutters (single-masted)
Schooners (two-masted)

By mid-September the sloop-of-war burst like a bombshell on the coast of Nova Scotia. Slipping innocently into Canso Harbor, the Yankee ship surprised and seized three English fishing vessels. From them it was learned that the main fleet was quartered at Madame Island, just across the bay. There some twelve ships were lying

The frigate *Constitution* in Boston Harbor.

at anchor while more than three hundred fishermen were engaged in salting down their catch.

The surprise was complete. In dismay the fishermen saw themselves condemned to spend the winter on that bleak, storm-beaten shore. But Captain Jones struck a bargain with them: if they would put nine of their ships into condition for immediate sailing, he would spare the remaining three to carry the men back to their homes. Should they refuse, however, he would be forced to burn all twelve vessels and leave the crews marooned, to make out as best they might through a bitter winter.

The fishermen flung themselves into the task with a will. When they had finished, Captain Jones kept his word and saw them safely home. Then after burning all the shore installations, he sailed away with his fleet.

It was at this point that John Paul Jones made what was perhaps the most important single capture of his career: the British merchantman *Mellish*. The ship was carrying a full company of English infantry, officers and men, who were at once made prisoners of war. But the crowning stroke of good fortune was her cargo: ten thousand heavy winter uniforms intended for Burgoyne's army. What a boon they would be to the half-clad soldiers of George Washington, who, even then, was planning to lead his tattered army against the Hessians at Trenton.

By this time so many prizes had been taken that Captain Jones had barely enough men to sail them into port, and none at all to fight if need should arise. He had

Boston Harbor.

effectively destroyed the fishing industry of the enemy. More important, the suddenness of his raid on Nova Scotia had caused such panic that echoes of it soon were heard in London.

Weary but triumphant, laden with spoils and glory, the gallant Captain led his astonishing fleet home, dropping anchor in Boston Harbor with only two days' water and provisions left. Eight enemy ships had been burned or sunk, nine others brought in as captives. A total of seventeen prizes within six weeks.

Nothing like it had been known before.

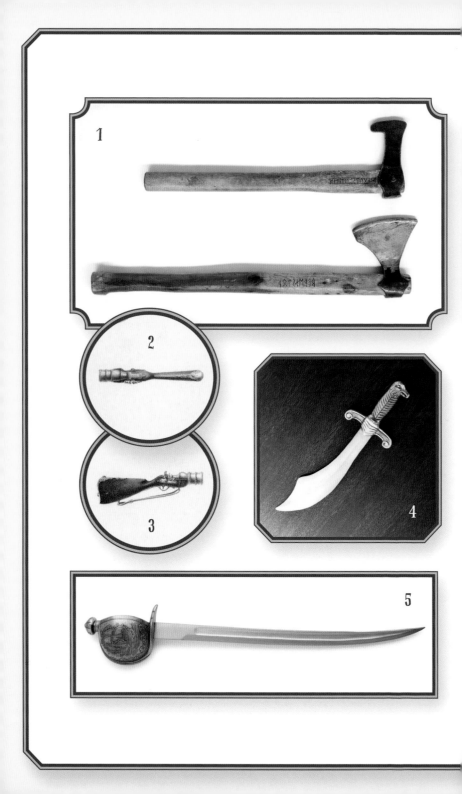

★ WEAPONS ★
USED BY THE AMERICAN NAVY

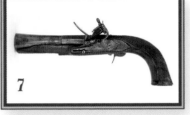

1. Axes
2. Launcher
3. Blunderbuss
4. Cutlass
5. Sword
6. Cannon
7. Blunderbuss
8. Flintlock pistol
9. Muskets

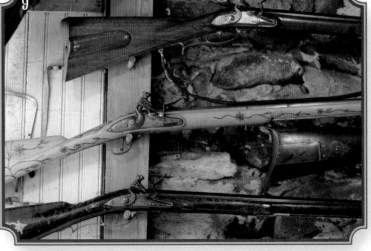

CHAPTER FIVE

A PLAN OF ACTION

Now occurred one of those ironic events that marked the life of John Paul Jones: he was relieved of command of his ship! It seemed unbelievable, yet it was true.

Commodore Esek Hopkins, in charge of building thirteen frigates, had appointed a new list of captains. They were men who, in most cases, had never fought a naval engagement. Once the first ranking lieutenant in the navy, John Paul Jones now found himself without a ship. So much for Esek Hopkins.

British General Burgoyne surrendering his sword to General George Washington after the Battle of Saratoga. New York, October 17, 1777.

For Captain Jones, fresh from a series of daring exploits, this was a bitter blow. It was next to the disgrace of being dismissed from the service. He felt that he deserved better of his adopted country. But the quality of the man which makes him unforgettable is that in just such moments, when his ship seemed to be sinking, he really began to fight. All the world was to learn this in the near future, but there were few who suspected it then. He determined to confront the Marine Committee in person and, as a captain whose commission had been signed by John Hancock, *demand* a ship of his own.

A crisis had been building during Jones's absence. The Colonies were in turmoil. The American cause seemed to be lost, and with that conviction men in office were losing their heads. Joseph Hewes had lost his battle for re-election. Benjamin Franklin was in Paris, asking the French king to support the Colonies. Jefferson was occupied in Virginia, while for some months it seemed that Robert Morris had been the entire United States Government. Times looked black indeed. In such a stew-pot of confusion and intrigue, who could be bothered with a brazen sea captain from North Carolina?

Thus months of evasion and delay were allowed to slip by before Congress passed the following resolutions:

RESOLVED,   That the flag of the thirteen
United States be thirteen
alternate red and white stripes,
and that the Union be thirteen
stars, white on a blue field,

	representing a new constellation.
RESOLVED,	That Captain John Paul Jones be appointed to command the ship *Ranger*.

The young Captain hurried at once to Portsmouth, New Hampshire, where a sloop was being made ready for sea duty. He found that most of her crew had been scraped together out of privateers. Only the loyal Jared Folger remained of his former officers. Jones had, moreover, to guarantee out of his own pocket a year's wages to the men. But at least he had a command.

Fortunately at this crucial hour a messenger brought splendid tidings. General Burgoyne had surrendered! John Paul Jones was ordered to carry the news with all speed to Benjamin Franklin, the American Commissioner in Paris.

It was the end of October, 1777, when the *Ranger* weighed anchor and stood out to sea. Jones drove his ship like a man possessed. He chose the northern stormy route because it was shorter, and cracked on sail until the older hands predicted that "the papers were being carried to Davy Jones." The hard-pressed crew was on duty eight hours and off four. The Captain himself seemed never to sleep. He was everywhere at all times, seemingly untouched by exposure or fatigue. But no one complained. All understood the urgency of the great news which the ship carried: *Burgoyne had surrendered.*

Thirty-one days after leaving Portsmouth, the *Ranger* dropped anchor in the River Loire, below Nantes. The young Captain hurried by coach to Paris, to place his dispatches in the hands of the American Commissioner.

Printer, inventor, statesman, herb-doctor, and philosopher—jack-of-all-trades, master of each and mastered by none. Such, at the age of seventy-two, was Benjamin Franklin. His lofty ideas and shabby wardrobe were already famous throughout Europe.

In keeping with his simple habits, Franklin shunned the luxurious Court of King Louis XVI. He lived in a quiet house just outside of Paris. Here it was, at the hour of supper, that Captain Jones found the old man of wisdom. The two had never met, yet they were already well known to each other. Wrapped in a faded dressing gown, with a black satin skullcap on his domelike head, Doctor Franklin cut something of an unusual figure; but behind steel-rimmed spectacles his eyes were vital and young, shrewd but kindly, missing nothing.

"I have been waiting for you," the old man told Jones at once.

Taken aback, the other demanded, "But how could you have known of my arrival, sir? I came with all haste—"

"In this country the very paving stones carry tales," the doctor said blandly. "The walls have eyes to spy. The doors have ears to listen. But come—what news do you bring? That at least is still a secret."

Jones blurted out, "General Burgoyne and his whole army are prisoners of war, sir!"

For a moment the old man remained silent, his eyes alight. Then he said, "This is what I have been hoping for, even though I reminded myself that he who lives upon hope will die fasting."

"Burgoyne was a brave man," the other grudged.

"No doubt," Franklin agreed. "But bravery in a poor cause is the height of simplicity, my friend. But remove your jacket, Captain. Set it by the fire to dry. Come, we shall sup together. It is possible to eat and converse at the same time." Agile as a cricket, the old man led the way to a table that had been set before a fireplace and laid with two covers. "Tell me—are you the possessor of a liberal fortune, Captain?"

Jones smiled. "Scarcely that, sir."

"I thought as much," the doctor chuckled. "That is why I asked you to sup with me. When a poor man dines at his own expense it is bad policy. Never dine out, young man, when you can dine in."

A servant entered with a tray, and Jones discovered that the meal consisted of one dish: mutton boiled with peas. A decanter of colorless liquid was placed at the doctor's elbow. Then the servant retreated, closing the door with care. Franklin listened attentively for the sound of diminishing footsteps.

Then he said, "Permit me to fill your glass, Captain."

"Is it white wine, sir?"

"Of the very oldest vintage. I drink your health and success in it, my friend."

After one sip, the guest exclaimed, "Why, it's plain water!"

"Plain water indeed." The old doctor wagged his head sagely. "And a very good drink for plain men. If you are poor, avoid wine as a costly luxury. If you are rich, shun it as a fatal indulgence." Franklin's eyes twinkled as he picked his way nimbly among words. "Eat your fill, young man, for there will be no pastry coming. Pastry is poisoned bread. Be a plain man. Stick to plain things."

John Paul Jones helped himself to a generous portion. "Your notions, doctor," he said, "coincide with my own. But I despair of achieving your wisdom."

"There are no gains without pains," came the answer. "And remember—as Poor Richard says, 'God helps them that help themselves!'" Suddenly serious, Doctor Franklin leaned toward his guest, and now his voice dropped to the note of a conspirator. "These be grave times, Captain—for France as for America."

"Is King Louis not yet ready to recognize the Colonies as a free nation?" Jones asked bluntly.

"Burgoyne's surrender may go far toward helping the King make up his royal mind," the doctor mused. "But it occurs to me that if a certain John Paul Jones could prove to the English that their seaports might be successfully attacked, it would have a tremendous effect on our Louis." The old man watched the light leap in his visitor's eyes. "Have you never given thought to such a possibility, Captain?"

"Have I not!" Jones exploded. "I've dreamed of it, planned for it! Give me a proper man-o'-war and in less than a month you shall hear glorious or fatal news of John Paul Jones."

Ben Franklin, with fur hat, in Paris.

"Ah! Tell me now, just what would you do with such a ship?"

"I'd teach the British that Captain Jones, though born in Britain, is no subject of their King, but an untrammeled citizen of the universe. I'd teach them that if they continue to ravage the American coasts, their own are just as vulnerable as New England's."

John Paul Jones came slowly to his feet. For a moment his eyes, so true a gray, had the look of the seer who comes to grips with a vision.

"Everything is lost through this timidity called prudence," he cried. "War should be carried on like a typhoon. Only statesmen back and fill, like cat's-paws in a calm."

"Fine words, Captain," Franklin murmured. "But have you an immediate plan of action?"

The flag of the thirteen colonies.

Brest Novr 5th 1778.
Recd Novr 12. 1778

I had the pleasure of writing you my dear Sir the 31st Ulto inclosing a Bill of Lading for 15 Whds. of Porter — I believe it will not be amiss to reserve one of them for me as it is highly probable that I may this Winter fit out at or near Nantes if a suitable ? can be found. — I have at last found means to purchase, and should be glad to hear of a very fast sailing Frigate of from 36 to 40 Guns. — I impati wait the result of your enquiries in consequence of my last.

I thank you for your favor of 27th Ulto — you before me circumstances which can be best seen thro' by the candid Eye of Friendship whose conne always merit attention. — I am not ill pleas that you can discover a Species of inflexability i my nature which will not suffer me to kneel a the feet of haughty Power, or to stoop where I cannot also esteem. — I know that this turn of Mind is highly Unfavorable to any who would Obtain Court favor or promotion in Europe; ye

A letter from John Paul Jones to Jonathan Williams requesting a ship in 1778.

"That I have!" came the swift assurance.

"I am all ears."

"It's like this, sir," Jones explained. "The Earl of Selkirk is a counselor and particular friend of King George. He is the laird of St. Mary's Isle, where I was born. I know every inch of that coast. I propose to seize the noble lord and take him back to America as a hostage. I'll not harm a hair of his head—but he'll have a price pinned on his coat-tails, like any slave up at auction in Charleston. With such a hostage, King George might come to terms."

"A bold scheme, young man. But would it work?"

John Paul Jones's teeth flashed white. "God helps them that help themselves, sir," he answered. "I have it on excellent authority."

The good doctor chortled. "You fellows so ready with the tongue are apt to be sharp with the steel. Would God I had been a man of action rather than a man of words. I'd sign aboard your ship myself!"

Rising, Franklin pattered toward the door. There he bent for a second in an attitude of listening. Reassured, he returned to the table.

"Hark well to what I say," he whispered. "The Duke of Chartres is King Louis's chief counselor. The Duke is also my friend. Though on the brink of war with England, no declaration has yet been made by France. I shall bend every effort to see that your *Ranger* is properly equipped. The Duke, if anyone, can persuade the King to sanction the sailing of an American man-o'-war against England. The rest is up to you."

The old man rose, stood for a moment lost in thought. "This is a time of greatness," he said slowly. "And I believe there is more than a touch of greatness in you, John Paul Jones. One day, men will look back and remember." A smile of extraordinary sweetness crossed the wrinkled face. "You must be weary, my good friend. You shall pass the night under my roof. Tomorrow retrace your steps to Nantes. A messenger will be sent to you at earliest opportunity. May he bring good tidings!"

In a flash of gratitude that left him humble, John Paul Jones knew that in this venerable man he had found a friend whose loyalty would never waver. The grip of his hand was warm.

"I shall now light you to your room, Captain," the good doctor was saying. "Ah, here is a book—a small pamphlet with which you may pass an hour."

While Franklin lighted a candle, Jones glanced at the slender volume that had been thrust into his hands: *Poor Richard's Almanac.* Opening it at random, his eyes fell upon a marked line. This is what he read:

"So what signifies waiting and hoping for better times? We make these things better if we bestir ourselves."

A laugh broke from John Paul Jones. Here was a man after his own heart! "Thanks are beyond me, sir," he said. "But you may count on me to bestir myself. Good night and God rest you."

"To you the same, my friend."

Doctor Franklin was as good as his word. Within a week the following message, signed by the American Commissioner, was delivered:

> The Duke has won his Majesty's consent. We advise you, after properly equipping the *Ranger*, to proceed in the manner you shall judge best for distressing the enemies of the United States, by sea or otherwise, consistent with the laws of war. We rely on your ability, and therefore give you no particular instructions as to your operations.

Here was an order exactly to John Paul Jones's liking. He was now a free agent, answerable to none.

Repairs to the *Ranger* went ahead with all speed. The sloop was to be disguised as a merchantman, presenting a broad drab-colored belt all around her hull. Thus, under the solemn cloak of a Quaker, she concealed the heart of a buccaneer. But her Captain was determined on one point: before setting out to attack the coast of England, he would see the new flag of the United States saluted by France!

It happened that events played right into his hands; for as the sloop got under way, she was met by a French squadron commanded by Admiral La Motte Picquet, top-ranking officer of the King's fleet. Jones himself hoisted the new American ensign to the masthead; and as the Stars and Stripes floated on the air he ordered a thirteen-gun salute. There was a moment's anxious pause; then came the answering *boom* of the Admiral's flagship. This was the first time the Stars and Stripes had been recognized among the flags of nations.

In high spirits, John Paul Jones headed the *Ranger* north toward the Irish Channel, into the teeth of a gale. And presently such an uproar was to arise in Britain as that island had not experienced in the almost two hundred years since the Spaniards bore down upon it with their Invincible Armada.

It was curious that John Paul Jones should have chosen Whitehaven as first in his plan of attack. For it was from this same port, just across the bay from his birthplace, that as a boy he had set out on his adventures.

The *Ranger* was now off the coast of Wales, running between Ireland and England, into the inmost heart of the British waters. Like young David of old, armed with but a slingshot, John Paul Jones would beard the British giant of Gath. A bolder enterprise could scarcely be imagined. It was the act of one who made no compromise with danger or death.

Jared Folger, suddenly leveling his glass toward the Irish coast, announced a large sail bound in. The sloop at once gave chase. Soon, almost within sight of Dublin, the stranger was overtaken, manned, and turned round for France. Jones then brought his ship about, passing the Isle of Man toward the Cumberland shore, arriving within sight of Whitehaven about sunset. By dusk the *Ranger* was hovering off the harbor with a party of volunteers ready to go ashore. But the wind shifted and blew fresh with a violent sea.

"I'll not call on old friends in such foul weather," Captain Jones decided. "We'll cruiser about and leave our cards here in a day or two."

The following morning, on the south shore of Scotland, the sloop fell in with a revenue cutter. It was the practice of such craft to board merchant vessels. But the cutter, scenting danger, took to flight, her two lugsails staggering under a heavy wind. Pelted with a hailstorm of shot from the *Ranger's* pursuing guns, the enemy managed to escape. Now the fat was in the fire!

The next afternoon, off the coast of Galloway, Captain Jones found himself so close upon a barley-freighted coaster that, to prevent her spreading the tidings of the *Ranger's* presence, he dispatched her with the news, stern-foremost, to Davy Jones's Locker. Her crew was picked up and saved. From them it was learned that a fleet of thirty ships lay at anchor in Loch Ryan. Captain Jones pointed his prow in that direction, but at the mouth of the Loch the wind again turned against him and he was compelled to abandon the project. Not before he had encountered a brigantine from Dublin, however, which he sank to prevent further intelligence.

Thus the *Ranger* hovered like a thundercloud off crowded harbors, darting like a bolt of lightening hither and thither—into the land-locked heart of the supreme naval power on earth. Off Carrick Fergus, on the Irish coast, a fishing boat (deceived by the Quaker-like innocence of the sloop) came off in full confidence. Her men were promptly seized, their craft sunk. From them it was learned that the man-of-war *Drake*, twenty guns, lay at anchor in the roadstead. Here would be a prize indeed! The sun was already setting as the *Ranger* stood in toward the land.

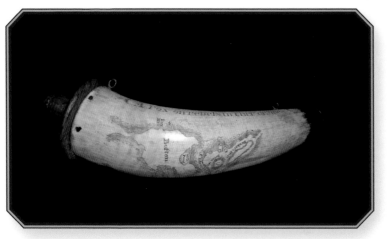

Cow horn gunpowder flask, made in Concord, Massachusetts.

"Surely, Captain," muttered Jared Folger, "you're not going right in among them? Why not wait till the *Drake* comes out?"

"Have confidence, my friend," the other retorted. "Perhaps I shall abduct the *Drake*."

Like any peaceful merchantman, the *Ranger* slipped into the harbor under easy sail. She drifted toward the unsuspecting warship, her anchors ready to drop and grapnels to make fast. She came to stand not a stone's throw from the enemy.

Calmly answering the man-of-war's hail, John Paul Jones whistled cheerily and gave orders for slipping the cable. And then, as if he had accidentally parted his anchor, he turned his bows on the seaward tack—his object being to crash suddenly athwart the *Drake*'s bowsprit, so as to have all her decks exposed at once to his musketry. The plan itself was perfect; but once more the winds intervened. A heavy squall came up, causing the Captain to make sail and beat a retreat.

Nevertheless, John Paul Jones had actually brought his sloop to anchor within hailing distance of an English man-of-war. He had answered hail and retired without arousing the least suspicion of his true purpose. At dawn, no one in Carrick Fergus knew how closely the Devil had passed that way during the night.

The rising sun found the *Ranger* midway in the channel at the head of the Irish Sea. England, Scotland and Ireland were all in sight. As far as the eye could reach, the Three Kingdoms were covered with snow.

All that day the sloop bore southeast toward Solway Firth. What memories that distant shore evoked in the mind of the lean, whip-strong man who paced the quarterdeck! It was as if time had stood still, and once more a boy named John Paul heard his uncle's prophetic voice saying, "Who knows? God may one day grant ye the honor o' striking a blow for the brave lads—yer ain clansmen—who fell to Cumberland's men on that bloody ground . . ."

Paul Jones snapped shut his telescope. "Mr. Folger," he said, "the time has come to leave our cards at Whitehaven. 'Tis many a year since I have stepped on that shore. Tell me, Lieutenant, have you ever driven spikes?"

"Spikes, sir?" the other echoed, baffled. "Why, yes, sir—"

"That is to say, into a cannon?" Jones persisted.

"Why, no, sir. Can't say as I have." What in thunder was the Old Man up to now? he wondered.

"Then this is as good a time to learn as any," came the answer. "Fetch me a hundred spikes from the carpenter. I'll have them in a bucket, if you please. And a brace of hammers—one for each of us."

Still mystified, Folger departed to carry out the order.

By dusk, the lighthouse on the promontory near Whitehaven came into view. Night stood on as the *Ranger*, undetected, glided on a light wind into the mouth of the harbor. Preparations for a landing party had already been worked out. John Paul Jones saw personally to the lanterns, the cutlasses and firearms. In his mind the plan of action was glass-clear. Whitehaven boasted some seven thousand inhabitants, defended by a fort on a hill behind the town. With twenty-nine men in two boats, it was the Captain's plan for one party to spike the fort's guns, while the second party set fire to the shipping in the harbor. All this must be accomplished before daybreak, while the unsuspecting townsmen were asleep in their beds.

Half a mile offshore the *Ranger* came quietly to anchor. With a soft splash the two longboats dropped into the water. Noiseless as cats the men took their places. The lanterns were carefully shielded. Not a sound was heard except the muffled oars in the rowlocks. All was darkness save for the intermittent light from the lighthouse. Like mysterious mammals the two boats eased through the black water toward their goal.

Not a light shone in the houses, but in the harbor the masts of some three hundred ships could be seen dimly against the stars. Whitehaven was a coal-mining town and the ships were colliers that carried the coal to London. Now, with the tide at full ebb, their dark hulls lay half out of the water and grounded, like so many beached whales. This too was part of Jones's careful plan. Behind the stranded fleet loomed the fort, its ominous batteries guarding the beach.

It was a long pull against a strong ebb tide, and as the boats ran into the shallows the sky in that high latitude was already streaked with dawn.

"Easy now, men," Jones whispered. "Not a sound to betray us! Every man knows his orders. Let no one fail me."

The Captain's boat landed square at the foot of the fort, while the second craft swung away toward the colliers. Leaving two men to stand guard, John Paul Jones advanced cautiously toward the fortress. How many memories of youth this harbor held! As a boy, John Paul had played on the dark battlements confronting him. Now, as a man, it was all different. Above his head the black gunports gaped like missing teeth, and in the starlight he caught the gleam of enemy guns. How alert would the sentinels be? Clutching the bucket of spikes and the hammers he beckoned to Jared Folger to follow.

Three other men, with muskets primed, covered the advance.

"Make haste, Mr. Folger!" Jones muttered. "Your shoulder for a ladder."

Without mishap the Captain scaled the mossy ten-foot wall. Up went the bucket of spikes. Silently the other men followed their leader. They found themselves on the parapet of the fort, ringed about by heavy guns that were all run in and ready for firing. At the door of the guardhouse Jones drew up short. Through a slit of window in the sentry box two guards could be seen lost in sleep and snoring mightily. In a matter of seconds both men had been gagged and securely bound. They came to in terrified surprise to find themselves prisoners. Descending into the guardhouse Jones and his men quickly subdued the token garrison who, likewise, were soundly sleeping.

"Easy enough so far," muttered Captain Jones grimly. "Now follow along as I go. A spike for every cannon. We'll tongue-tie these noble pieces so they'll never speak again."

From gun to gun John Paul Jones and Jared Folger passed, driving home into each touchhole the silencing spikes. Thirty-six cannon in all were quickly put out of commission.

When the clang of the hammer had ceased the Captain straightened up, wiped his sweat-streaked face. "Look to the harbor, Mr. Folger. See if the ships are afire."

The lieutenant climbed the parapet. "Not a spark, sir," he announced. "And scarce an hour till sunup—"

"What ails the blundering dolts?" Jones exploded. "We'd best get back to shore. Something's gone awry." He glanced down at the two sentries, staring wide-eyed at their captors. "We'll leave the rest of the spikes with you, my lads," he grinned. "Calling cards for His Majesty."

On shore, the rest of the crew was discovered to be in confusion. It seemed that in the very instant of firing the ships, the lanterns had gone out. No one had thought to bring a tinderbox.

One of the men grabbed Jones by he arm. "Captain," he pleaded, "'tis madness to stay here longer! Look ye—the sun comes up. The whole town will be at our throats!"

A pewter
tankard.

Jones shook the man off. "Coward!" he thundered. "Get me a spark somebody—just one spark! The sun takes care of itself."

Someone proffered a stump of pipe half filled with tobacco. Jones seized it. As always, he shone in the very moment of defeat. Disposing his party so as to retreat at an instant's warning, he raced across the cobbled square toward the nearest house. From some good citizen of Whitehaven he would get a spark to kindle all of Whitehaven's habitations in flames!

Pipe in mouth, Jones knocked loudly on a door.

A window flew open. An angry voice shouted from within,

"Begone with you, beggar! To wake a man at such an hour—be off!"

"Morning finds you lazy, good sir," Jones chided. "The sun is up and you should be likewise. I beg only for a light for my pipe. Quick, open up!"

A rusty lock groaned. A grumbling fellow in a nightshirt stood aside as John Paul Jones stalked rapidly to the fireplace, raked aside the cinders and lit his pipe. Before the sleepy townsman could collect his senses, the stranger had vanished.

Meantime, a dozen other pipes had been produced and as many sparks were ready for their work of destruction. In the gray light of dawn the black hulks of the stranded colliers were now clearly visible.

Approaching from windward, John Paul Jones turned to address his men. "Ten of you stand by the boats," he ordered. "The rest of you follow me. We'll set a conflagration in England that will end all future burnings in America! Step lively, lads, and keep your pipes alight."

Like phantoms the silent men swarmed up the sides of the listing ships. Hurrying below decks they broke open lockers and seized great bunches of oakum, dry as tinder, and leaped into the steerage. The glowing tobacco struck fire. Tar pots were emptied to fuel the flames. As Jones retreated up the forward hatchway, he saw volumes of smoke billowing up from a dozen other ships. An offshore wind sprang to further his purpose.

By this time, the men who had been left to stand guard shouted that the townspeople were aroused. The first vanguard of sleepy citizens, hastily clad, came crowding toward the pier. Confusion stamped their faces. Several among them had seized buckets of water, thinking to put out the fire which, of course, they believed to be of accidental origin. They were not long deceived.

For John Paul Jones, cutlass in hand, sprang to meet them. "Back, you sheep!" he thundered. "The first among you to advance another foot will know the taste of my steel!"

Stupefied, the crowd stood motionless, as if it had struck down roots. Who was this wild-eyed fellow, who faced them like an avenging angel? This armed enemy who stood upon the sacred soil of Britain with none to strike him down? A rising note of panic spread from lip to lip. Mighty pillars of flame, catching the rigging and spiraling through a forest of masts and spars, were shooting skyward.

It was time for Jones's men to retreat.

"Into the boats, lads! Our work is done."

Without opposition from the townspeople the men climbed aboard, while Jones covered their retreat with his cutlass. Then the captain leaped into the stern sheets.

Not until the boats were well out into the harbor did the citizens of Whitehaven remember the fort. They quickly discovered that their precious guns were no better than so much iron in the ore. At length they managed to fire a rusty old 4-pounder that lay on the beach. In their excitement, however, they fired without discretion and the shot fell short. John Paul Jones's men crowed with victory as they clambered aboard the *Ranger*. In jig-time the anchor was weighed, sail set, and the sloop was swinging jauntily out to sea.

John Paul Jones—the first man since William the Conqueror to invade England and come away unscathed—looked back at the mighty conflagration. Had the wind been stronger, not a ship or a house could have escaped. His Britannic Majesty had been shown that wanton destruction on the American coast could be brought home to his own doorstep.

Best of all, not one drop of blood had been spilled.

CHAPTER SIX

"BEAT TO QUARTERS!"

But this amazing cruise had just begun. The *Ranger* now stood over the Solway Firth toward the Scottish shore, where St. Mary's Isle shimmered in the sun. At noon on the same day, with twelve seamen and Jared Folger, John Paul Jones landed half a mile from the manor house of the Earl of Selkirk.

The stately mansion stood in the midst of a park, half hidden by hedges of clipped boxwood and yew. Smoke drifted lazily upward from its many chimneys. No one challenged the advance of the landing party. Stationing

Even today, tea is important to many cultures, and a silver tea service is a coveted item (James Tissot, 1836–1902).

his men silently round about the house, John Paul Jones sounded the silver knocker that gleamed on a dark-paneled door.

An elderly servant responded.

Captain Jones said boldly, "I would speak with the Earl of Selkirk, if you please."

The servant stared, wide-eyed. Surely this outlandish sea-going figure, with so forward a tongue, had never been seen in St. Mary's Isle! "The master is in Edinburgh, sir," came the faltering reply.

"Ah, sure? Is your lady within, then?"

The servant's glance fell on the cutlass, the brace of pistols thrust jauntily into a belt. This stranger had the speech of a gentleman, and yet—"Yes, sir," came the stammering answer. "Who shall I say it is?"

"A gentleman who calls to pay his respects to this illustrious household." Jones whipped a scrap of paper from his pocket and scribbled his name. Then he strode past the servant into the wide hall.

As the doors of the drawing room opened, a lady rose from a chair before the fire—a slim figure dressed in rich brocade. John Paul Jones drew up short. He had expected to be confronted by some haughty matron; but the lady who stood before him was barely more than a girl. Her fair hair fell to her shoulders in soft ringlets. A necklace of rubies, bright as pigeon's blood, gleamed against the whiteness of her throat. And for a second John Paul Jones stared back at her, disarmed. It came to him that in her person was the warmth that had never touched his childhood; the vision of beauty he had known must exist somewhere, but that he had never beheld until this moment. With an effort he collected himself.

The Countess of Selkirk glanced uncertainly from the paper which the servant had placed in her hands, to the lean man in blue, holding himself so rigidly before her.

"Who may it be that I have the honor to receive?" she queried.

The Captain bowed from the waist. "Milady," he said, indicating the slip of paper, "my name is in your hands."

"Which leaves me equally ignorant, sir," came the cool reply.

The man smiled wryly. "A courier dispatched to Whitehaven this morning, milady-Countess, could bring you more particular tidings as to who I am!"

The lady drew herself up. "You speak in riddles, sir. State your errand at once!" she commanded.

"Your ladyship—" and John Paul Jones advanced a step—"I come to see your husband, the Earl, on a matter of urgent importance."

"You have chosen a poor moment to arrive," the Countess informed him. "My husband is in Edinburgh." She reached toward the bell-cord, as if to summon assistance.

"One moment, I pray," the man begged. "Do you give me your word of honor that what you say is true?"

"Is it possible, sir, that you question my word?" A note of unbelief ruffled the proud voice.

"A thousand pardons, milady," the man said. "I would not impugn your lightest statement. But it occurs to me that you may have suspected the object of my visit. In which case, you would surely seek to shield your husband."

For the first time a hint of alarm crossed the Countess's face. She moved nearer to the door. "Sir, I do not dream what you mean by this intrusion—"

A smile of rare charm lighted the Captain's face, instantly reassuring the woman who confronted him. "It is regrettable, milady," he was saying, "that in the profession of arms a man is sometimes driven to an action he deplores. I have the honor of being an officer in the American Navy. The purpose of my visit was to seize your husband as a hostage for the Colonial cause. Since I have your word of honor that the noble lord is not here, I shall take my leave." John Paul Jones bowed gallantly, straightened up. "But disappointed though I am, our interview has given me the opportunity of standing in your gracious presence. This is a moment I shall not forget."

"Can this really be true?" gasped the Countess, her hands fluttering to her lips.

"From your window you may see the sloop-of-war which I have the honor to command," Jones told her. "Permit me to salute your ladyship's hand and depart."

Scarcely realizing what she did, the Countess extended her hand. John Paul Jones raised her fingers to his lips, bowed twice and quitted the room.

Outside, he found his men waiting in angry impatience over the delay, with Jared Folger trying vainly to pacify them. Briefly Jones informed them of the Earl of Selkirk's absence.

"There is nothing for it, men," he stated, "but to weigh anchor and be off at once."

A rumble of discontent went through the crowd. "With nothing for our pains?" growled a sullen voice. "This be war, Cap'n. What manner o' fighting is this?"

"And what, pray, would you have?" demanded Captain Jones.

"Some silver plate, to be sure," came the surly answer.

"Are we pirates," Jones protested, "or honorable seamen in the American Navy?"

Another of the men stepped forward. "Have you forgot the enemy in America, sir?" he challenged. "They help themselves to whatever they want, with no by-your-leave."

"There are always some who use the King's livery as a disguise," Jones said. "The rest are men of honor—even as ourselves." But he understood that these rough seamen were not to be readily turned aside. In their sight, war was war! Belay all this nonsense about King's livery and honor! These particular men, moreover, were the most efficient in his ship. Here was no moment to stir up a mutiny. There were bigger matters afoot than silver plate.

John Paul Jones made his decision. "Mr. Folger, I place these men in your charge. Under no circumstances are they to be allowed to enter the house. Their demand shall be made to the Countess through you. Only such objects as her ladyship chooses to offer may be taken away. Is this understood?"

Jared Folger touched his hat. "It is, sir."

"Excellent. I shall hold you, sir, personally responsible."

John Paul Jones swung on his heel and retraced his steps to the waiting boat.

The Countess of Selkirk, however, was more than a little confused to receive Mr. Folger's demand. She retired at once; but presently the old servant appeared carrying a silver tray with a magnificent tea service.

Satisfied with their haul, the seamen seized the plunder and departed. By the time they had regained the ship, John Paul Jones was engaged in writing his famous note to the Countess of Selkirk:

Madame—After so courteous a reception, I am disturbed to make you no better return than you have just received from the actions of my men. Unfortunately my profession of arms leaves me no choice in the matter.

But permit me to assure you, dear lady, that when the plate comes to be sold, I myself will be the purchaser! The silver will be safely restored to you as soon as possible thereafter.

I go now, Madame, to fight His Majesty's ship *Drake*, lying at Carrick Fergus. Dare I dream that the lady-Countess will offer up a prayer for one who, coming to take a captive, has himself been captivated?

Your ladyship's adoring enemy

— John Paul Jones.

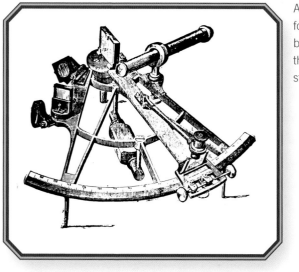

A sextant, used for navigation by measuring the angle of the stars.

Many months later, at great expense to himself, the Captain made good his pledge: every piece of stolen plate was restored to its rightful owner.

Wearing an English Jack at the main-t'gallant masthead, the *Ranger* stood out of the Solway Firth and pointed her sharp bows once again toward the Irish Sea. Her ports were closed to hide the guns with their lighted matches ready for instant battle. Folger and his men went from gun to gun, cleaning out the touchholes with oakum, refitting the tompions lest spray get down the muzzles. By the time Carrick Fergus hove in sight, the sloop was in fighting trim, her men likewise.

Scanning the shoreline with his glass, Jared Folger discovered a large ship—possibly the *Drake*—standing out into the channel. "They're dropping a longboat now, sir," he said, handing over the telescope.

Jones's eyes danced. "We'll decoy that boat alongside, Mister. Take the helm yourself and hold our stern toward the enemy. Make sure they don't take a sight on our broadside."

The longboat stood on, smartly rowed by half a dozen oarsmen. A British officer in the stern sheets was examining the *Ranger* through a glass. Presently came the hail, "Ahoy! What ship are you?"

In a broad Scots brogue, the better to further his deception, Jones shouted back, "The *Gilnockie* of Kirkcudbright. I'm short o' men. Ye'll nae find any press aboard *this* ship."

"Heave to and lower a ladder," called the British officer. "I'm coming aboard to search."

"Come aboord and be hanged to ye!" Jones shouted back, elated at seeing the enemy play so unsuspectingly into his hands. "Ye'll nae find what ye seek!" To his own men he muttered, "Keep well below the bulwarks, lads. Every musket primed to cover the boarding party. We'll salt this boatload of herring away in jig-time."

As the longboat swung up under the brig's counter, the Britishers shipped their oars and the officer climbed the ladder. Barely had he topped the bulwark rail when his eye fell upon the rows of cannon mounted on the maindeck, and a score of Yankee sharpshooters with muskets held at ready. The Englishman's jaw dropped.

"Welcome to the American sloop-of-war *Ranger*," said Captain Jones affably, advancing. "I am John Paul Jones, commanding officer. I believe that my name is well known in Whitehaven." At this the officer flushed up, and Jones added, "A handsome sword you're wearing, Lieutenant. You will allow me—?"

The British officer fumbled to remove his sword. "I see that I am your prisoner," he said stiffly.

"Aye, but you'll not want for company," came the genial answer. "Order your men aboard, sir, and no nonsense!"

Under the leveled muskets of the marines, the sailors clambered sullenly aboard. Their boat was cast adrift. "So you are John Paul Jones, the pirate?" the lieutenant said coldly. "We had word of you last night by express from Whitehaven. You understand, sir, that when the King's men lay hands on you, you'll be hanged like a highwayman."

Jones chuckled. "I make no doubt your King would be delighted to see me dangling on a gibbet. But I shall spare him that pleasure as long as possible."

Suddenly a gun boomed from the distant *Drake*—a signal of recall for the longboat.

"Ah," smiled Captain Jones, "His Majesty waxes impatient. Mr. Folger, will you escort these gentlemen below? The *Drake* is standing toward us and will engage presently. I trust, Lieutenant, that you and your men will not be too uncomfortable in the bilge. 'Tis a pity, sir, that I must deprive you of the opportunity of seeing a King's ship royally trounced."

With sour looks the lieutenant and his men followed their captors below.

The wind was right under the land and the *Drake* was

working out slowly while the sloop, with a fresher breeze, tacked to and fro in the channel.

When at last the enemy man-of-war had fairly weathered the point, Jones allowed her to approach within hail. Loud and clear across the waves came the *Drake's* challenge, "What ship is that?"

"Your enemy!" came the trumpeting cry. "The American sloop-of-war *Ranger*. Open fire—if you dare. We're waiting for you."

"She's hoisting her colors, sir," murmured Jared Folger.

"I can see that, Mister. Lower the Jack. We'll give them the Stars and Stripes!"

As a huge St. George's Cross broke from the enemy's gaff, Jones himself sprang to the locker and attached the American ensign to the halyards. The wind caught it instantly, and for a second the Captain stood enveloped in its bright stripes and spangles. And through him stormed the thought, "I first hoisted this flag on an American ship. If I perish tonight the name of John Paul Jones shall live!" The blood was singing like warm wine in his veins; he felt vibrant and alive to the very tips of his fingers.

"Beat to quarters, Mr. Folger."

"Beat to quarters it is, sir."

The drums went roaring through the ship while the marines—fine riflemen from Maine and New Hampshire—swarmed aloft into the tops.

"Back the main-tops'l, Mr. Folger," sang out the order. "Let the enemy close! Stand by, larboard battery. Aim high for her crosstrees."

The sun was shining behind the green hills of Ireland as the distance between the two ships rapidly diminished. Mounting twenty guns to the *Ranger's* eighteen, the *Drake* was heavier built and higher riding than the American sloop. To the keen eye of John Paul Jones these seeming advantages were drawbacks; for while he owned an immense respect for the stout oak planking of English ships, their proportions were invariably so awkward that they seemed to have been built by the mile and chopped off as required. The British method of fighting was to lie alongside the enemy and battle it out. The *Ranger* would be no match against such tactics. Captain Jones determined first to cripple the enemy's speed, then lie off and rake her decks at his pleasure.

"Hard up the helm, Mr. Folger. Square the yards!"

At once the sloop fell away before the wind, which brought her smartly athwart the bows of the oncoming man-of-war. Now within easy rifle shot, the *Drake's* towering masts were all in a line, her canvas and rigging fair target for a raking broadside. The sloop's gunners were straining madly to train the muzzles of the 6-pounders on the enemy's crosstrees.

"*Fire!*"

Down came the glowing matches. The *Ranger's* battery burst into flame. The guns leaped back in their breechings. Round-shot screeched through the air. It ripped the *Drake's* rigging from bowsprit to mizzen. Holes gaped in her canvas. Her foretopsail swayed and fell in a tangled web of ropes.

Without headsails, the warship now could run only

John Paul Jones at battle.

before the wind. From the moment of that first crippling broadside John Paul Jones knew that this initiative lay wholly with him. Yet he did not make the mistake of underrating his opponent. Not for nothing was the *Drake* a British man-of-war, with the traditions of the Royal Navy behind her. Her officers were certain to be men of experience. Her crew could scarcely number less than one hundred seventy-five disciplined seamen.

Fearful of being again raked, the *Drake* had fallen off from the wind on a course parallel to the *Ranger's*. Now broadside to broadside, both ships let go at the same time with a full volley. But the Britisher, firing hastily, was swinging off the sloop's larboard quarter, causing most of her shot to miss the mark. Robbed of her headsails, she was becoming unmanageable, while the *Ranger* spun and pirouetted around her—playful as a yearling colt.

Yelling like dervishes Jones's men leaped at their smoking guns to sponge out, load, and send the carriages flying back to battery. It was for this that their commander had drilled them so ceaselessly. Three broadsides were being fired to every one from the *Drake*. In the face of such punishment, the enemy's topmen were unable to get aloft to repair the damage done to rigging and canvas.

The British were following the tradition of firing low into the enemy's hull. But John Paul Jones had little fear of being sunk immediately. Striding back and forth behind the smoking battery, shouting encouragement to his men, he felt certain that he would have the *Drake* battered to a hulk long before his own ship could be seriously distressed.

At close range now both ships were exchanging Broadsides. Nothing could be heard above the deafening thunder of the guns and the rumbling of the carriages. Streaked with sweat, barefooted on the sanded decks, the *Ranger*'s men hauled desperately at tackles and rammers.

Suddenly, on a lucky roll, the enemy found the target. A hail of cannon balls smashed into the sloop's bulwarks. Timbers splintered. The *Ranger* shuddered to her keel-bolts. Gunners were knocked spinning. The cries of the wounded shrilled above the din.

"Keep those guns firing!" bellowed Captain Jones.

It would never do to let the enemy get in another such broadside. Satisfied that the *Drake*, crippled as she was, could no longer work to windward, John Paul Jones ordered the forecourse spread, thinking to haul forward and there rake the enemy's bows once more.

"Hard alee!"

Instantly the sloop, like a race horse obedient to the flick of a heel, shot away to starboard, rapidly outdistancing the enemy. By the time the *Ranger*'s wounded had been carried below and the guns again loaded and run out, the sloop had forged well ahead of the *Drake*, to find herself on the warship's weather bow.

Jones's eyes flashed with triumph. "Now we've got her where we want her, men," he shouted, and to the helmsman, "Wear ship!"

The *Ranger* came down running free, slipping diagonally across the enemy's bows, at the same moment discharging a thunderous broadside. She came about instantly, returning on the opposite tack, opening up for the first time with her starboard battery. What havoc! The *Drake*'s masts and spars were hanging like jackstraws. Her riddled canvas ballooned as it dragged in the sea. She was completely at the mercy of John Paul Jones, who had out-sailed and out-fought her gallant commander so unmercifully.

Blackened by powder-smoke, with sweat blinding their eyes, the *Ranger*'s gunners never ceased firing, while the marines in the tops rained a hail of shot upon the enemy's quarterdeck. The British captain tottered and fell. His first lieutenant collapsed beside him. A final broadside from the sloop smashed into the enemy's forward bulwarks, dismounting the guns in that quarter and tossing the gunners into the sea. The *Drake* swung slowly broadside, helpless as a hamstrung beast.

Then from across the waves sounded a hoarse cry: "Quarter! In God's mercy—*quarter*!"

"Cease firing, men!" cried John Paul Jones. "The enemy strikes!"

Down from the stump of the *Drake*'s mainmast fluttered the tattered Cross of St. George. The battle was over. It had lasted one hour and four minutes.

The man-of-war was a floating wreck. Not a mast or spar remained intact. Her rigging was a hopeless tangle, her sails in shreds. Forty-two of her crew were laid out, dead or disabled, while the *Ranger*'s losses were two killed and six wounded.

John Paul Jones was determined to take his prize back to France. Obviously he must get away as soon as possible, for the Irish Sea was really a British lake and as soon as word of the battle spread, half the Royal Navy would descend to avenge the *Drake*'s defeat.

Fortunately the night was mild, the sea calm. By daybreak the wreckage had been cleared away, a prize crew put aboard the doomed ship. Then with the British man-of-war in tow, the victorious *Ranger* stood out through the North Channel, bound for everlasting glory.

• CHAPTER SEVEN •

VICTORY

News of John Paul Jones's triumph spread through–out Europe. Almost overnight the name of the Scottish gardener's son became a household word. In France, King Louis and the gracious Queen made much of him at Court. Benjamin Franklin was as delighted as a small boy. Even his enemies were silenced.

Then the incredible happened: for the second time John Paul Jones was relieved of command. A newly built frigate, the *Alliance*, arrived from America. The captain, a Frenchman named Pierre Landais, brought word from the Continental

Vue d'optique showing a naval battle during the Revolutionary War between John Paul Jones of the *Bon Homme Richard* and Captain Richard Pearson of the British naval vessel *Serapis*, September 22, 1779.

Congress that the *Ranger* was to return at once to Boston. For her Esek Hopkins had appointed a new captain. With death in his heart Jones watched the ship that had grown so dear to him set sail for home, under another man's command.

The War of Independence was dragging on. One by one the Colonial ships were being sunk by the enemy while John Paul Jones was allowed to cool his heels in France—a man without a country.

It was Benjamin Franklin who came finally to his friend's assistance. King Louis was persuaded to outfit a squadron of nine vessels and appoint the young Captain as commodore of the fleet.

The flagship proved to be the *Duras,* an East Indiaman of ancient pattern, half of whose timbers were unsound. For armament Jones was obliged to accept forty cannon so old that they had been doomed by the French Navy. But at least the *Duras* was a command and from that fact John Paul Jones took heart. The ship's name he promptly changed to *Bon Homme Richard*, in honor of Franklin's *Poor Richard's Almanac.*

Upon the loyal Jared Folger fell the burden of signing a crew. Since it was against the laws of the land for a foreigner to recruit French sailors, Folger was forced to accept the riffraff of all nations: Maltese, Portuguese, Malays and Arabs. Surely here was the worst crew that ever a man-of-war set forth with. Who would have guessed that such men would one day fight like tigers?

Jones was heartened to learn that the frigate *Alliance* would be one of his fleet. Fortunately he did not know that Pierre Landais was a scoundrel who, at the end, would turn downright traitor. The captains of the other ships were Frenchmen, fiercely resenting the Yankee upstart who had been shown such favor by the King.

But in spite of the annoyance, the intrigues and delays, Jones was tireless in his efforts to whip the squadron into shape. By August 14, 1779, the fleet cleared the roadstead off the Ile de Groix. And with the knowledge that he was at last free of the shore—of its conniving politicians and spies—John Paul Jones's spirits went soaring. He was at sea again! True, his ship was sluggish in answering helm; his crew was unpredictable, his officers untried. He had no real authority over the other captains, who stubbornly maintained their independence. By all the rules of logic he was whipped before he went into battle. But it is just this fact which singles John Paul Jones out from the vast army of the forgotten: not until the odds were hopelessly against him did he really begin to fight.

During the first night at sea, six ships of his squadron deserted. Who could say why? Scarcely out of sight of the French coast, the fleet was reduced to the *Bon Homme Richard*, the *Alliance*, and the *Pallas*. Such a catastrophe might have disheartened any other captain; but it was in this crisis that John Paul Jones planned one of his most daring exploits.

The Cheviot hills on the Scottish border were in sight. In the distance ships could be seen standing in for the Firth of Forth, on whose south shore lay the port of Leith. Jones resolved to make a dash at Leith and force the town to pay ransom or lay it in ashes. He called the captains of the other two ships to explain his plan of attack. Cottineau, of the *Pallas*, approved the scheme. But Pierre Landais instantly opposed it.

"*Par bleu!*" the Frenchman fumed. "Have you lost your senses? Edinburgh Fort is on the Firth. We could not pass under those guns and remain afloat."

Patiently Jones explained that the very boldness of the scheme assured its success. The enemy would never expect him to sail under the muzzles of the mightiest fortress in Great Britain. Not until a shrewd appeal was made to Landais's greed, however, did the Frenchman consent to be a party to the plan. Jones promised that no less than 200,000 pounds sterling should be demanded of Leith as ransom. The thought of sharing one-third of such a staggering sum brought Landais into the fold.

Along both shores of the Firth, the panic caused by the three approaching ships spread like wildfire. The suspicious vessels had so long lain off and on, that few doubted they were commanded by that same notorious pirate who had set Whitehaven aflame. The alarmed citizens of Leith hastily threw up batteries. Arms were obtained from the neighboring castle of Edinburgh. Alarm fires were kindled. Yet so cleverly did Jones conceal the warlike intent of his ships that more than once they were hailed as merchantmen by passing vessels.

The little squadron stood on until it was almost within cannon shot of Leith. A storm was making and Jones scanned the darkening skies anxiously. How often had the elements conspired against him! But despite the threatening skies he completed preparations for the assault upon the town. Pyramids of round-shot were piled about the guns; the boats were cleared for landing, boat-crews fold off, small-arms issued. The forbidding fortress commanded the entrance to the river and through his glass Jones could make out two tiers of mighty guns.

Impatiently he paced the quarterdeck as he waited for the turning of the tide. In his wake stood the *Alliance* and the *Pallas*, and heaven alone knew at what moment their two commanders might turn traitor, even as the others had done.

What Jones feared came to pass: as the tide turned, the wind shifted directly down the Firth. At the same moment an electrical storm of great violence burst upon land and sea, heeling the ships hard down. The squadron was powerless to make headway. Under such conditions the attack on Leith was hopeless.

In utter dejection of spirit John Paul Jones signaled his two convoys to come about and stand out before the gale. Bitterness filled him. Must he return to France, without fighting a single battle, and confess his failure? How his enemies would crow over his downfall! What would Benjamin Franklin say? He would never be given a chance to assemble another fleet. Jared Folger held silence, but his heart was sore for his beloved captain. And then John Paul

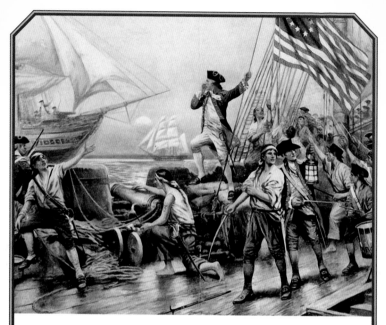

BATTLE COMMANDS

BEAT TO QUARTERS:
Give a signal, often by
drumbeat, to the crew to
prepare for combat.

CLEAR FOR ACTION:
Prepare the ship for combat.

HOIST THE COLORS:
Haul up the flag.

STRIKE THE COLORS:
Haul the flag down as a token of
surrender.

WEIGH ANCHOR:
Haul up the anchor.

In the battle between John Paul
Jones's sloop *Ranger* and the
British *Drake:*

RANGER
18 gun (cannon) sloop disguised
as a merchantman
2 killed, 6 wounded

DRAKE
20 guns (cannon)
42 men dead or disabled
200 men (and the ship)
captured

Jones's chin came up in the gesture of determination that Folger knew so well: he would woo good fortune not by despair, but by resolution!

And shortly luck—there is no other word for it— threw in John Paul Jones's way the crowning achievement of his life.

Weathering the gale that had driven them out of Leith, the three ships were standing bravely up the coast. By the following morning the wind had blown itself out. Rounding Flamborough Head, a fleet of forty merchantmen, protected by two British men-of-war, could be seen scarcely three miles to windward. Jones's heart pounded. Here at last was his chance for battle!

As distance closed, the warships could be recognized as the *Serapis* and the *Scarborough*. The former, a 50-gun frigate, was well known by reputation to Captain Jones. The fact that the Britisher's armament and man power far outweighed his own dismayed him not at all. The forty merchantmen, like so many chickens, were fluttering in a panic under the wing of the shore. But the two warships were standing on to do battle. Accepting the challenge at once, Jones signaled his consorts to lead the *Scarborough* off on a chase while he himself engaged the *Serapis*. With relief he watched the *Alliance* and the *Pallas* decoy the smaller of the two warships in the opposite direction.

"You may beat to quarters, Mr. Folger." Jones's voice was quiet, but a devil of anticipation danced in his eyes. "We are about to have the honor of engaging His Majesty's mightiest frigate."

Folger raised his trumpet. "All hands to clear ship!" he shouted.

A rousing cheer burst from the crew. Who were they to fight the bone and sinew of the King's Navy in a lumbering hulk of a ship? And who was he who stood so sure and straight on the quarterdeck to install this riffraff with such fervor, to blind them to such odds?

Bulkheads were knocked down, gunports triced up, the guns run out and loaded with double shot. All light sails were furled. Decks were wet down and sanded. The marines swarmed aloft with muskets and combustibles. The powder-monkeys tumbled over each other in their eagerness to provide cartridges. Grape and canister and dismantling shot were hoisted up from below. By the time the ship had been cleared for action, the red sun had sunk behind the Yorkshire Wolds and the Head of Flamborough was lost in blue shadow.

John Paul Jones was determined on close action. He would first clear the enemy's tops, and then her decks, that he might board her. The two ships moved slowly together through a deepening dusk, while the glow on the eastern horizon bespoke a rising moon. With battle lanterns lighted the *Bon Homme Richard* was running free to cover the single mile that separated her from the enemy. Glancing astern, Jones discovered that although the *Scarborough* was still in pursuit of the *Pallas*, Pierre Landais's ship had disappeared from sight: a deserter on the eve of action before ever a gun was fired.

From the quarterdeck Captain Jones had a final word for his crew. "Remember, men," he cried, "that for us there can be only victory. We fight with a gallows-rope around our necks. God willing, we shall make the enemy soon cry 'quarter'!"

An ominous silence enveloped the ship. The gunners peered anxiously through the gunports at the ghostly frigate whose masts and spars were silvered by the first light of a rising moon. Then across the darkening waters came an imperious hail: "What ship are you? Answer at once or I fire!"

Up to the peak of the ensign staff raced the Stars and Stripes. At the same instant rose John Paul Jones's triumphant answer: "Your enemy! Fire and be hanged to you!"

Down came the glowing matches and the entire larboard battery of the *Bon Homme Richard* roared out. But almost at the same second a red streak of flame shot skyward and the ship trembled to her keel-bolts. A fiery wind swept the decks. There came the rend and splinter of wood. Ropes and blocks tumbled to the decks like thudding bodies. Moans and shrieks filled the night. Out of the pandemonium emerged the ship's carpenter, blood pouring from a gash on his face. In a wild voice he was crying that the 18-pounders had burst, killing half the gun-crews and blowing up the deck above them.

What followed was a nightmare. The enemy's broadside belched forth a rain of fire. The *Serapis* was a clean sailer, her commander a man of great skill and courage. He nosed his ship ahead, then dropped back, each time raking the American with a murderous broadside; while the *Bon Homme*

Richard, with braces shot away and half her armament destroyed, answered helm laboriously. The two ships were so close together that a biscuit could have been tossed from one deck to the other. Again and again the broadsides thundered out, filling the darkness with sound and fury.

The Yankee crew of all nations fought like tigers as one after another of their guns were silenced. Jones saw one man whip off his shirt when a gunner called for a wad, while another snatched the rammer from the hands of the officer who staggered with a grapeshot in his chest. What was it that held such men to their stations when only a lunatic could have hoped for victory? What but the certainty that at the fiery heart of the inferno stood a man who swept aside all obstacles, into whose mind the thought of defeat could not enter?

By this time both ships were aflame in a dozen places. Wood-smoke poured out of the *Bon Homme Richard*'s hold, shot through with powder fumes. Flaming shreds of canvas and rigging fell upon the naked shoulders of the straining crews. The Yankee marines, standing their ground in the tops, riddled through they were by enemy bullets, maintained a brisk and deadly fire.

Pierced again and again through the hull, the *Bon Homme Richard* was leaking badly, but suddenly a lucky slant of wind pulled her ahead. Jones threw the helm hard over, causing his vessel to strike the *Serapis* on the larboard quarter. He saw his jib boom crash into the enemy's rigging and shouted for boarders to grapple. But the grappling irons failed to hold and the other ship came free, falling off behind the American.

With three feet of water in the hold Jones's ship was foundering. Her cannon were almost completely crippled, half her gunners dead or wounded.

Black with powder-smoke, Jones drew a hand across his eyes. "Mr. Folger," he croaked hoarsely, "we must close with the enemy at all costs. Issue small-arms to your men. We are going to board."

"Small-arms it is, sir," cried the other, leaping to fulfill the command.

Once more the wind came to Jones's salvation, allowing him to wear ahead and round the enemy's bows. At this moment, a third ship appeared out of the darkness to windward. Recognizing it as the *Alliance*, Jones gave a shout of relief. Help at last! The cowardly Landais was returning to lend aid. The *Alliance* came up swiftly, with all sail set and shining in the moonlight. But her contribution to the battle was to pour a broadside into the stern of the *Bon Homme Richard*. This was followed with a round of grapeshot. Frantically Jones sent up signals. Had Landais gone mad? Did he know what he was doing? Before passing off to leeward in the darkness the Frenchman fired a final treacherous broadside. The blow, so cruelly dealt, crippled the tiller of the *Bon Homme Richard* and wounded a score of men, among whom was Jared Folger.

At that moment came a shuddering jolt as the anchor fluke of the *Serapis* hooked into the stays of the American

Portrait of John Paul Jones by George Matthews, circa 1890.

ship. With his own hand Jones sprang to lash the two ships together. Side by side, locked in death grip, both vessels tore at each other's vitals. Above the thunder and din of battle rose the agonized shrieks of the wounded and dying. Jones saw his own ship settling deeper and deeper, with flames shooting upward into the rigging. A cannon ball snapped off the flagstaff above his head and the Stars and Stripes trailed in the water. As in a daze he heard a hoarse shout from the enemy: "They've surrendered!"

A British officer was bellowing through a trumpet, "Do I understand that you have struck?"

"Struck?" Jones thundered defiantly, flinging up his head. "By the Power, no! *I have just begun to fight!*"

The words roared like a wind through the ship. It was no new message. The British had heard it as they climbed the bullet-swept slopes of Bunker Hill. Washington had rung it in the ears of the Hessians on a snowy Christmas morn at Trenton. But rising above the thunder of the ships' guns that September night, the dauntless words put new heart into the faltering, told the dying that they had not fought in vain.

The British were hacking at the lashings that bound their ship to the American. If the *Serapis* could once get free, her heavy guns would put an immediate end to the battle. But the Yankee marksmen in the tops picked off the ax-men with deadly precision. It was at this moment, through the heat of the battle, that John Paul Jones noticed the enemy's hatch—partly open. An idea burst like a rocket in his brain: a grenade dropped into that opening could force an immediate surrender . . .

Though wounded, it was Jared Folger who clambered to the maintop with a bucket of grenades. Sixty feet above deck, he slid out on the yard. The open hatch was a small target, scarce two feet square . . . The first grenade hit the deck of the *Serapis* and spat venomously. The second also missed fire. But the third curved swiftly over the hatch, closer and closer, to disappear into the dark opening.

It fell among the powder-monkeys. Instantly the night was rent by a tremendous explosion. The mainmast of the *Serapis* cracked and tottered, swung this way and that on its loosened shrouds. With a vast sigh it disappeared overside. Cannon were tossed into the air like toys. Stout oak planking shredded into flaming splinters. Men with their clothing on fire leaped screaming into the sea. Then through the smoke of battle the British commander himself could be seen fumbling at the color halyards. Slowly the Cross of St. George was lowered. No one saw the enemy marksman who aimed his rifle at Jared Folger, still high up on the yard; but everyone saw the lifeless body of the youth from Nantucket plunge into the water. For Jared Folger, as for all the others, the battle of the *Serapis* and the *Bon Homme Richard* was at an end.

A sorry procession of high-ranking British officers filed aboard their enemy's sinking ship. Their once-fine uniforms were grimed and torn. The gardener's son from Solway Firth stood at the gangway to receive them. And perhaps in that moment (who knows?) time flashed backward and John Paul became a boy again, hearing his uncle's bitter voice say, "God may one day grant ye the honor o' striking a blow for yer ain clansmen, who fell to Cumberland's men on that bloody ground. . . ." All his life had been a preparation for this triumph. But as the English commander advanced, offering his sword in token of defeat, John Paul Jones shook his head. A half-reluctant admiration shone in his eyes. His teeth flashed white in a blackened face. His voice was husky as he said, "I'll not accept the sword of any man who has so bravely defended his ship. But I would be proud to offer you a glass of wine, sir!"

On the *Bon Homme Richard* lay sixty-seven dead, one hundred six wounded. On the smoking *Serapis* were eighty-seven dead, one hundred thirty-four wounded. Jones's ship was beyond salvage and sinking fast. He ordered all his men and prisoners to be transferred to the British man-of-war. With head uncovered he watched the Stars and Stripes float from the enemy's gaff, with the Cross of St. George upside down below the young Colonial ensign.

Offering up a silent prayer for Jared Folger, for all the others who had fallen so gallantly, John Paul Jones turned to look for the last time upon the ship that had served him so well. The *Bon Homme Richard* went down head-foremost with all sail set—t'gallant sails, royals and moon-rakers—every rag of canvas that a ship would wear. As the dark waters parted to receive her, the jack-pennant she had worn so jauntily in action seemed to cry, "Hail! Hail and farewell!"

JOHN PAUL JONES RETURNS TO AMERICA—IN DEATH

Upon the discovery of Jones's body in a Paris apartment only two weeks after his 45th birthday, French authorities laid him to rest in a lead-lined coffin filled with alcohol, expecting that the Americans would honor him with a formal return to America. But Governor Morris, the American ambassador to Paris, disliked Jones and refused to pay to return the body to America, or even to pay for an honorable funeral in Paris. The French, however, respected Jones, and saw to it that he received a dignified burial. Within three weeks, though, the massacre of Protestants by French revolutionaries saw hundreds of bodies buried in a mass grave next to Jones's burial site. Soon, records of the exact location of the burial site were lost in the turmoil of twenty-five years of revolution.

More than one-hundred years later, Horace Porter, a Civil War brigadier general, arrived in Paris, seeking to find the remains of the United States' first naval hero. After several years of research, Porter in 1905 narrowed in on the likely location and obtained permits to excavate. After finding and ruling out many human remains, Porter found a lead coffin containing a corpse, and later examination showed that it held a remarkably well-preserved body, 5 feet 7 inches in height. This, along with battle scars and the presence of the damaged lung known to have killed John Paul Jones, identified the remains as that of the American hero.

On April 24, 1906, President Theodore Roosevelt honored John Paul Jones in a ceremony attended by many dignitaries. Jones's final resting place in a crypt beneath the Naval Academy chapel in Annapolis, Maryland, took place on January 26, 1913.

The final resting place of John Paul Jones.

AFTERWORD

Here, in the crowning moment of his life, it is fitting to take leave of John Paul Jones. On his return to Paris he was wildly acclaimed. Honors were heaped upon him. His fame soared across land and sea. Louis XVI presented him with a gold-hilted sword and made him a Chevalier of France. For him Marie Antoinette had a miniature painted in her likeness. The Continental Congress, somewhat belatedly, sent a gold medal in recognition of his triumph.

But the rest of the story is soon told. He was to learn how quickly a hero may be forgotten.

Catherine the Great.

Though it's not well known, John Paul Jones had an entirely new chapter to his career after leaving the US Navy. After missing out on an appointment to a new ship, and finishing service in Europe, on April 23, 1787, he entered into service to Empress Catherine the Great of Russia.

He served as rear admiral on the flagship *Vladimir*, a 24-gun vessel, in the Black Sea, fighting against the Ottoman Turks. He helped the fleet repel the Ottomans from the area, but as had been the case in the United States, John Paul Jones alienated some of his colleagues, and turned the Russian commander Grigory Potemkin against him.

Soon, Jones was recalled to St. Petersburg, where he remained idle while rival officers plotted against him. At one point, an improper relationship with a young girl caused a scandal, though in the end it was proven that most of the scandal was created by his political enemies.

Although he received awards from the Russian leadership, he never served aboard a ship again and left Russia in July of 1788. For a time, he considered serving for Sweden, but in the end decided against it and returned to Paris, where he would soon die.

The Colonies seemed to have no further need of him. Benjamin Franklin was recalled to America. Joseph Hewes lay dead. No ship was offered for the command of this man who, more than any other at sea, *had humbled* the proud enemy and brought the War of Independence closer to victory.

Catherine the Great of Russia invited John Paul Jones to command her Black Sea fleet. He was appointed an admiral. But credit for his victories was stolen by subordinates who sent false reports to the Empress. Jealous officers schemed to have Jones recalled. Catherine quickly lost all faith in him. A bitterly disillusioned man, John Paul Jones returned to Paris.

He was at the end of his resources. Years of exposure to the elements had sapped his strength. Desperately ill, no longer a hero, he found himself friendless, penniless and alone. At the age of forty-five he died. His unmarked grave in the St. Louis Protestant cemetery soon became buried beneath the rubble on which tradesmen built their shops. For one hundred years its dust lay undisturbed.

In 1908, the American ambassador to France began a systematic and successful search. A fleet of warships carried the leaden coffin home. Today, in the crypt of the splendid chapel at Annapolis, John Paul Jones—the small boy of twelve who had set out from Whitehaven so bravely on his adventures—lies at final rest.

All his life had been a fight.

VOL. LXX, No. 6   1905   PRICE, 35 CENTS

THE · OCTOBER ·
CENTURY
· MAGAZINE ·

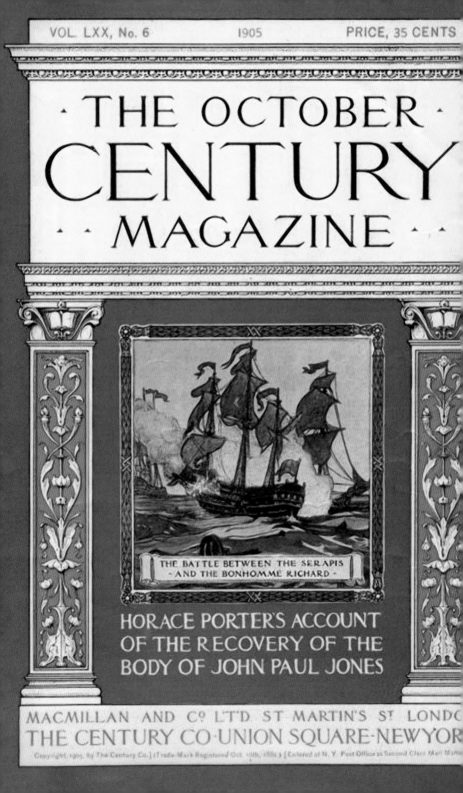

THE BATTLE BETWEEN THE SERAPIS
· AND THE BONHOMME RICHARD ·

HORACE PORTER'S ACCOUNT
OF THE RECOVERY OF THE
BODY OF JOHN PAUL JONES

MACMILLAN AND C⁰ LT'D ST MARTIN'S S⁺ LONDO
THE CENTURY CO·UNION SQUARE·NEWYOR

THE MAN AND THE MYTH

When the infant United States needed a fearless sea captain to harry the British at sea, John Paul Jones was the man both skilled and brave enough to do it. His bold deeds earned him the honor of being called father of the US Navy. But how much of his life is legend and how much fact? Did he really shout, "I have just begun to fight!" in the battle with the *Serapis*? Imagine the deck of his ship slippery with blood after a battle at close quarters. The ship is sinking, his men don't know if he is alive or dead. Confusion reigns and the flag appears to be coming down. Did anyone stop to

Popular magazine published in 1905.

record the captain's response to the British when they asked if the ship had struck? Probably not. But what is certain is Jones's indomitable spirit. He would never give up and his actions are proof of his thoughts if not his exact words.

The planned kidnapping of Lord Selkirk and the appropriating of the family silver is another famous incident in Jones's career. But how much do we really know about Jones's conversation with Lady Selkirk? We do know that the teapot still had warm tealeaves from breakfast when the sailors took the silver to the ship and we also know that the tealeaves were still there when Jones returned the silver seven years later. Jones himself wrote letters about this episode. John Paul Jones was a self-made man who modeled his life on the code of chivalry. We know how important it was to him to be considered a gentleman—especially with regard to a lady of the aristocracy.

John Paul Jones was a indeed a hero—one who led his crews into the fray and even more importantly inspired colonial leaders with his victorious battles at sea.

IN THE MOVIES AND MUSIC INDUSTRY

John Paul Jones as a character is mentioned or briefly depicted in many movies about the Revolutionary War. Only one major movie tells his entire life story, though the movie is sometimes slightly criticized as being overly sensational.

In 1959, director John Farrow made a movie with Warner Brothers studio about the life of John Paul Jones that featured some big Hollywood names at the time, although they may not be familiar to modern audiences. John Paul Jones himself was played by actor Robert Stack, veteran of more than forty movies and many television programs. Another famous actor of the time, Charles Coburn, played Benjamin Franklin, and Bette Davis had a small role as Catherine the Great, for whom John Paul Jones served near the end of his career.

The poster for the movie was seen by a young musician of a band called Led Zeppelin. John Baldwin was the new bass player at the time, and when a friend saw a poster of the movie *John Paul Jones*, he suggested that John Baldwin use this name for his stage name. Thus, John Paul Jones joined Jimmy Page and Robert Plant in one of the most famous rock and roll bands of all time.

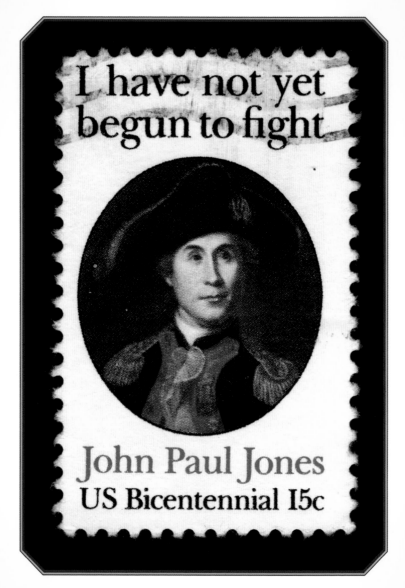

A postage stamp, circa 1979, bearing John Paul Jones in honor of the United States Bicentennial.

John Baldwin, bass player for one of the most legendary rock bands of all time, Led Zeppelin, was inspired to use John Paul Jones as his stage name.

Opposite: John Paul Jones wearing the typical uniform of a United States Navy officer in the late 1700s.

Above: An advertisement for clothing, 1919.

★ CAST OF CHARACTERS ★

JOHN PAUL JONES

The United States' first acknowledged naval hero. Sometimes referred to as "Father of the United States Navy."

JOSEPH HEWES

North Carolina representative to Continental Congress and later Secretary of the Navy. Appointed John Paul Jones to command the North Carolina ship.

GENERAL JOHN BURGOYNE

British general who lost the Battle of Saratoga. John Paul Jones brought news of this defeat to Benjamin Franklin in Paris.

PICQUET DE LA MOTTE

French naval admiral. Exchanged gun salutes with John Paul Jones in Quiberon Bay, France, marking the first time a foreign power recognized the United States Navy.

CAPTAIN RICHARD PEARSON

Captain of the HMS *Serapis*, Pearson was defeated by John Paul Jones and the *Bon Homme Richard*.

CATHERINE II OF RUSSIA

Ruler of Russia. She commissioned John Paul Jones to command the Russian Navy after Jones left the service of America.

JARED FOLGER

A character "invented" by the author; a composite of many loyal officers and sailors who served for John Paul Jones.

COMMODORE ESEK HOPKINS

Commander in Chief of the Continental Navy. Commanded John Paul Jones on 1776 Nassau mission. Later censured by Congress, and relieved of command in 1778.

HELEN HAMILTON DOUGLAS

Lady Selkirk, wife of Dunbar Douglas, 4th Earl Selkirk. While intending to kidnap the Earl of Selkirk, John Paul Jones instead met Lady Selkirk and allowed his crew to seize the family's silver.

BENJAMIN FRANKLIN

An American Founding Father who became John Paul Jones's acquaintance and mentor while in Paris in 1777.

KING LOUIS XVI

Ruler of France who honored John Paul Jones with the title of Chevalier in 1780 after Jones defeated British warship *Serapis*.

GEORGE WASHINGTON

Commander of the Colonial Army and later first President to the United States.

★ TIMELINE ★

1747
JULY 6:
John Paul is born in
southwest Scotland, to
John Paul Senior and
Jean McDuff.

1760
John Paul sails out of
Whitehaven aboard
Friendship. For the next
fourteen years he learns the
craft of seamanship while
working on merchant and
slave vessels.

1769
John Paul, while
commanding the *Betsy*,
survives a mutiny but
is forced to flee to
America, now with the
alias John Paul "Jones"
to protect his identity.

1775
OCTOBER 13:
Congress buys its first two warships,
the *Lexington* and *Reprisal*.
DECEMBER 7:
John Paul Jones is named first
lieutenant of North Carolina's official
ship of the colonial navy, the *Alfred*.
He raids the Bahamas while serving
for Commodore Hopkins.

1777
JUNE 14:
John Paul Jones is ordered by Congress to take command of the USS *Ranger* on a mission to France, with orders to attack British commercial ships.

1778
FEBRUARY 6:
Treaty of Alliance with France is signed.
APRIL 17:
Jones attacks British port of Whitehaven. On April 20, he captures HMS *Drake*. On April 23, he sets fire to a British fleet in Whitehaven.

1787
Jones joins the Russian Navy, where he fights in the Black Sea against the Turks.

1789
French Revolution begins.

1783
SEPTEMBER 3:
Revolutionary War officially ends with the Treaty of Paris.

1793
JANUARY 21:
King Louis XVI is beheaded.

1780
King Louis XVI of France knights Jones with title "Chevalier."

1792
JULY 18:
John Paul Jones is found dead in Paris.

1779
Jones earns respect of French and takes command of USS *Bon Homme Richard*.
SEPTEMBER 23:
Jones captures British warship HMS *Serapis*. This marks the high point, and virtually the end, of Jones's career with the US Navy.

1776
Jones assumes command of the *Providence*.

INDEX

Russian Navy and, 144, 145

strategy and, 68, 75, 88–89, 92

Jones, John Paul (Led Zeppelin bassist), 149, *151*

L

La Motte Picquet, Admiral, 94

Landais, Pierre, 123, 127–128, 132, 135

launchers, *80*

Led Zeppelin, 149, 151

Leith, 128–129

Lexington (warship), 40

Louis XVI, King of France, 86, 88, 123, 126, 143

M

Madame Island, 76, 78

man-of-war components, *50–51*

man-of-war jobs, 28

Marie Antoinette, 11, 123, 143

Marine Committee, 84

marines, 28

mates, 28

Maxwell, Mungo, 21–22, 23–24, 30

Mellish, 78

military strategy, 68

monkeys, 28

Morris, Governor, 140

Morris, Robert, 84

muskets, *81*

N

Naval Academy (Anapolis), 140, 145

naval commands, 130

naval jobs, 28

naval strategy, 68

naval weapons, *80–81*

Nichols, Captain, 55, 58

Nova Scotia, 75

P

Pallas, 127, 129, 131–132

Paul, John. *See* Jones, John Paul

Paul, William, 14–16, 20, 36

ABOUT THE AUTHOR

As a boy, Armstrong Sperry was captivated by tales of sailing ships and pirates. His great-grandfather was a clipper ship captain who told young Sperry exciting stories of his adventures with pirates in the China Sea. Armstrong Sperry himself enlisted in the Navy and later, still looking for adventure and fascinated by life at sea, he shipped aboard a copra schooner from Tahiti to Bora Bora.

With his love for the sea and his experience in the Navy, Sperry is the ideal author for the exciting tale of the father of the American Navy.

Armstrong Sperry was awarded the Newbery Medal for his book *Call It Courage*, a poignant tale of a young boy's challenges as a seafarer in the South Seas.

In this stirring adventure, Armstrong Sperry uses all his familiarity with sailing ships to bring alive the great sea battles that Jones fought in the early day of his adopted country's struggle for independence.

Sloop-of-war USS *Richmond.*